100

BEADED

JEWELRY
DESIGNS

100 BEADED
JEWELRY
DESIGNS

Easy-to-bead necklaces, bracelets, brooches, and more

Stephanie Burnham

INTERWEAVE PRESS

A QUARTO BOOK

Copyright © 2005 Quarto Inc.

Published in North America by

 INTERWEAVE PRESS

Interweave Press LLC
201 East Fourth Street
Loveland, CO 80537-5655, USA
www.interweave.com

Library of Congress Cataloging-in-Publication Data
Burnham, Stephanie.
100 beaded jewelry designs: easy-to-bead necklaces,
bracelets, brooches, and more/Stephanie Burnham;
editor, Christine Townsend. p. cm.
Includes index.
ISBN-10: 1-931499-99-3
ISBN-13: 978-1-931499-99-6
1. Beadwork. 2. Jewelry making. I. Title: One
hundred beaded jewelry designs. II. Townsend,
Christine, 1957- III. Title.
TT860.B87 2005
745.594'2—dc22
2005003705

QUAR.BSJ

Conceived, designed, and produced by
Quarto Publishing plc
The Old Brewery
6 Blundell Street
London N7 9BH

Project Editor: Liz Pasfield
Art Editor: Anna Knight
Assistant Art Director: Penny Cobb
Designer: Julie Francis
Copy Editor: Alison Howard
Photographer: Philip Wilkins
Illustrator: Kuo Kang Chen
Indexer: Pamela Ellis

Art Director: Moira Clinch
Publisher: Paul Carslake

Manufactured by PICA Digital Pte, Singapore
Printed by SNP Leefung Printers Limited, China

10 9 8 7 6 5 4 3 2

contents

introduction

I wrote this book to inspire people who want to create their own beaded jewelry. Complete beginners who have not previously attempted beading will find projects that are both easy to work and stylish to wear. There is also plenty within these pages to challenge more experienced beaders to take their work further and incorporate a personal sense of style and design. Most importantly, each project has been designed with clear instructions that can be followed exactly, or adapted to individual requirements.

As you flip through the projects, you'll notice that I've used many different materials, including natural elements like shell, slate, agate, and wood. You'll also see beads from Venice, Japan, China, and the Czech Republic, as well as several glass beadmakers in the United States and Britain. I love to use color, shape, and texture in my work. When I begin to design, I gather an interesting selection of beads and simply start to play. Then the magic happens, and a new design emerges. Try the same sort of magic for yourself!

Versatile designs
Pretty flower beads are the perfect choice for *Daisy Chain Necklace*, (see page 26).

A treasure trove of designs

100 Beaded Jewelry Designs is easy to use; it's divided into three main sections plus one on basic techniques. The first section, *Classic Lengths*, includes designs to suit every taste and incorporates lots of texture and color. Many of the pieces can be adapted to fit any neckline. The second section, *Chokers*, includes designs intended to be worn fairly high around the neck or, in some cases, just at the base of the neck. Designs range from classic pearl chokers to young, funky styles in strong fashion colors. Matching items complement some of the pieces. The lariat designs in the third section, *Lariats and Longer Lengths*, are made from a single length of beadwork and are worn by wrapping together at the front. The

lariat is one of the most elegant forms of necklace, and can give a casual or more formal look depending on the embellishment chosen.

Each of the designs is accompanied by a wonderfully clear photograph, as well as some of the best diagrams I have ever seen; in fact, many of the designs could be worked from these alone. A "Bead Store" panel accompanying each project contains all the information you'll need to select the correct beads, with examples shown to scale so you can simply place beads on top of the images to check the size.

Striking centerpiece
Blacklip Shell Necklace, (see page 51), is designed around a strong focal bead.

Picking up the basic techniques

The techniques section includes simple tutorials detailing how to work each of the different skills. If you have never tried a particular stitch before, working a practice piece is well worth the trouble, and will give you confidence before you begin the project. Each project includes step-by-step instructions to guide you through every stage of the design process. Take time to study the illustration as it will help you to establish how the design fits together. Never be afraid to change an element of the design to put your own stamp on your work.

Throughout the sections you will see my love of embellishment, color, and texture. All the pieces were a delight to design and make, and it is wonderful to see them brought together in such a diverse and interesting collection.

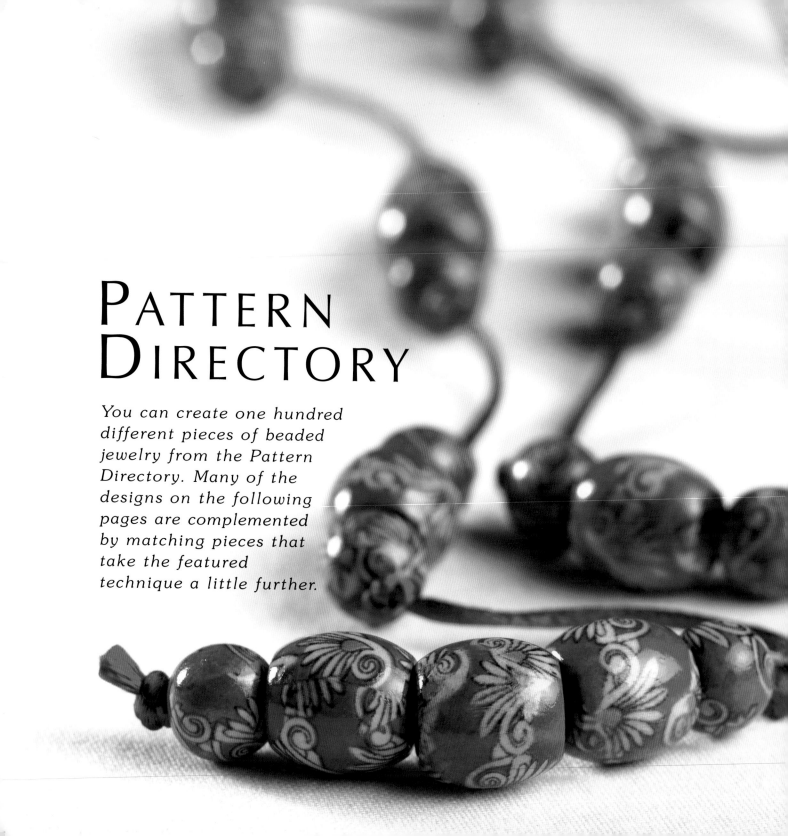

PATTERN DIRECTORY

You can create one hundred different pieces of beaded jewelry from the Pattern Directory. Many of the designs on the following pages are complemented by matching pieces that take the featured technique a little further.

how to use this book

This book has been designed for those who are new to beading and the more experienced beader. The three sections in the Pattern Directory contain many different designs suitable for all levels. The Techniques section provides useful information on all the basic skills required to create these beautiful and easy-to-wear jewelry pieces.

Each piece has been beautifully photographed.

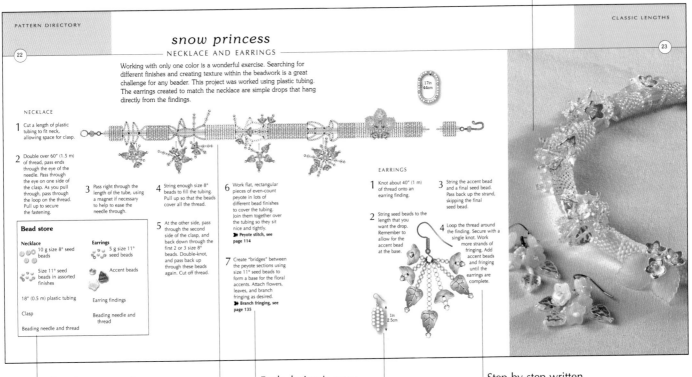

A bead store panel accompanying each project contains all the information you'll need to select the correct beads. Examples are shown to scale so you can simply place beads on top of the images to check the size.

Each design is cross-referenced to the techniques section.

A diagram shows the number and order of beads and where possible the position of clasps.

An illustration conveys the dimensions of the item of jewelry.

Step-by-step written instructions guide you through the project.

CLASSIC LENGTHS

autumn bronze

PENDANT AND EARRINGS

You can tell that this piece was designed to enhance the lovely focal bead. I chose the strap and tassel color carefully to complement rather than detract from this gorgeous bead. Clean, stylish lines make these earrings the perfect complement to the necklace. The stars hang from drops added to the base of the chain loop that forms each earring.

Bead store

Pendant

 15 g size 11° seed beads.

 25 star accent beads

Focal bead

Clasp

Beading needle and thread

Earrings

 5 g size 11° seed beads

 Five star accent beads

Earring findings

Beading needle and thread

PENDANT

1 Thread the needle using about 60" (1.5 m) of thread, leaving a 6" (15 cm) tail. Using the seed beads, work two lengths of single right-angle weave to comfortable choker length.
➤ **Right-angle weave, see page 129**

2 Stitch one end of each of the lengths together, using the center side beads of the last worked circle (right-angle weave) on each length of the straps. Do not cut thread.

18in
46cm

3 String the focal bead, then add enough size 11° beads to fill the length of thread inside the focal bead. This will add strength to the necklace.

4 Make a tassel at the bottom of the focal bead using strands of branch fringing. Work the longest strands first, then add shorter lengths to achieve the desired effect. Add stars to some of the "branches."
➤ **Branch fringing, see page 135**

5 Add short branch fringing to the top of the feature bead, using some of the single right-angle weave beads as anchors.

6 Attach the clasp. Sew stars to some of the strands of fringe.
➤ **Attaching a clasp, see page 140**

EARRINGS

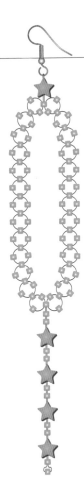

1 Work a chain 25 diamonds long using single right-angle weave, leaving an end about 6" (15 cm) long as for the necklace.
➤ **Right-angle weave, see page 129**

2 Bring the ends of the chain together. Join by working in and out of the top bead two or three times from each end, as for square stitch. Secure to the loop on the finding at both sides. As you work, loop around the finding so the beading hangs level with it. Leave the short thread in position for now.
➤ **Square stitch, see page 125**

3 Add the star drop by passing the thread down to the bead at the bottom center of the loop. Add 2 beads, then 1 star. Repeat three times. Add 2 beads. Take the needle back through the first of the drop beads, then the rest of the beads to the main body of the chain. Secure with a double knot. Take the needle through 2 or 3 more beads. Cut thread.

4 Return to the thread at the base of the finding. Add a star bead. Attach top and bottom to the nearest seed bead. Fasten off.

3in
7.5cm

pearl lozenge

NECKLACE AND BRACELET

These lovely lozenge-shaped pearl beads have a luxurious feel. The design they inspired is a different take on the traditional string of pearls. For an intriguing look, work the pearls used in this design on their ends. Use a two-strand clasp. You'll need to work the picot edge one side at a time so the bracelet will sit correctly. This design would also look good as a choker or lariat.

16in
41cm

NECKLACE

1 Thread the needle using about 60" (1.5 m) of thread, leaving an 8" (20 cm) tail. Attach to one side of the clasp using a double knot.

2 String 3 seed beads, 1 pearl, and 3 seed beads. Repeat until the necklace is the required length. String 3 more seed beads.

3 Remove the other side of the clasp from the one attached to the necklace. Pass the needle through its eye, then through the 3 seed beads and the last pearl bead added.
➡ **Attaching a clasp, see page 140**

4 String 6 seed beads. Pass the needle back through the first bead again, then through the next seed bead to make the first beaded loop.
➡ **Bead loops, see page 135**

5 Work two 12-bead loops. Finish with a 6-bead loop. Pass through the next pearl. Repeat in every seed bead section to end.

6 Pass the needle through the clasp. Turn, and work a final row of loops to complete.

REPEAT

Bead store

Necklace

15 g size 11° seed beads

25 to 30 pearl lozenge beads

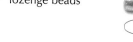
Clasp

Beading needle and thread

Bracelet

10 g size 11° seed beads

30 to 40 pearl lozenge beads

2-strand clasp

Beading needle and thread

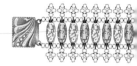

BRACELET

1 Thread the needle with 60″ (1.5 m) of thread. *String 1 pearl, 2 seed beads, repeat from *. Pass back through the first pearl to form a circle. Secure with a double knot between the pearl and next seed bead.

2 Pass through the 2 seed beads and the second pearl again.

3 String 2 seed beads, 1 pearl, and 2 seed beads. Pass back through the previous pearl, seed beads, and pearl added. Continue to required length.

4 Take the needle out of one side of the end pearl. String 2 seed beads, and pass through the eye on the corresponding end of the clasp. Pass back through the 2 seed beads, then down through the pearl.
➤ **Attaching a clasp, see page 140**

5 Repeat to attach the other side of the clasp. Secure by passing through the pearl and both ends of the clasp eyes several times.

6 Pass down through the seed beads and the first pearl again. String 4 seed beads. Pass back through the first of these beads to form a little picot. Pass through the pearl, the 2 seed beads, and the second pearl. Work to the end of the first side.

7 Repeat the picot edge for the second side.

8in
20cm

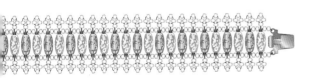

spice island

NECKLACE AND BRACELET

The hot colors of the spice trail islands, along with the animals of the African plains, inspired this set in shades of bronze and terra-cotta. The bracelet shows how a different base color can really change the look of a piece. It has shorter loops and contains more leaves, which when combined with the star accent beads, give a great textured look.

NECKLACE

1 Thread needle, using 60" (1.5 m) of thread. Attach one end of the toggle clasp.
➤ **Attaching a clasp, see page 140**

2 String 4 terra-cotta size 11° beads, then size 6 beads to the required length for the necklace. String 4 more terra-cotta size 11° beads. Pass through the other end of the clasp, and then back through these beads.

3 Working flat, fold the necklace in half. Pass through to the central size 6° bead. *String 20 terra-cotta size 11° beads. Pass back through the first bead to form a loop. Pass through 6 size 6° beads. Repeat from * three times.

4 Passing through 6 size 6° beads each time, work four more loops using 15 terra-cotta beads, then work loops using 10 terra-cotta beads to the end. Turn.

5 Pass through the first 2 size 6° beads and the next size 6° bead along from the first loop. String 15 bronze beads and form a loop. Pass through the next size 6° bead, string 20 bronze beads and form a loop. Pass through the next size 6° bead, and string a bronze bead and a leaf. Pass through the bronze bead, then the size 6° bead. To finish, string a bronze 15-bead loop, then a bronze 20-bead loop. You should be at the bead with the next of the initial loops. Repeat this process of making loops to fill in the spaces along the base of size 6° beads over the next three 10-bead loops.

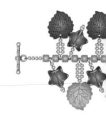

Bead store

Necklace

  10 g terra-cotta size 6° seed beads

 10 g terra-cotta size 11° seed beads

 20 g size 11° seed beads in bronze/ mahogany, mixed

22 to 30 acrylic leaf accent beads

21 to 25 animal-print star beads

Toggle clasp

Beading needle and thread

Bracelet
As the necklace but adapt quantities.

17in
43cm

6 Fill the 15-bead loops with spaces between the loops of 20 beads; 25 beads; a bronze bead and a leaf; 25 beads; 20 beads.

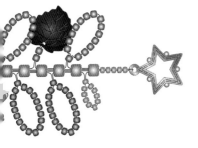

7 Fill the 20-bead loops with spaces between the loops of 25 beads; 30 beads; 2 bronze beads and a leaf; 25 beads; 30 beads.

8 Place stars at the center in the same size 6° seed beads as the original loops. String a terra-cotta bead, a star and a terra-cotta bead. Pass back through the star and the terra-cotta bead, and then back through the size 6° bead to where the next star is to be. Repeat for the other side.

BRACELET

Work the bracelet in the same way as the necklace, and follow the diagram below to complete.

7in
19cm

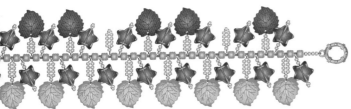

hedgerow

NECKLACE AND BRACELET

This fairytale duo is a riot of wonderful flowers, leaves, and accent beads. The central section is in an embellished spiral peyote stitch. A section of free-form peyote with different sizes and textures of beads completes the necklace. This technique is ideal for experimenting with texture and color.

NECKLACE: CENTER SECTION

1 Thread the needle with 60″ (1.5 m) of thread. String a size 11° seed bead and form a stop bead.

2 String 99 more seed beads. Work in peyote stitch, but adding 2 beads where, in the standard stitch, 1 bead is added. Let the beads fall gently to each side, making sure their holes face upward.
➤➤ **Peyote spirals, see page 117**

3 Work peyote stitch placing a green bead between each bead added on the previous row. Note that a bead is placed between each pair of beads.

4 Work in peyote stitch, adding 2 beads between each bead of the previous row.

5 Work as Step 3.

6 Work peyote stitch using size 8° beads.

7 Work a final row of single size 8° beads to produce a solid, slightly exaggerated edge.
➤➤ **Attaching a clasp, see page 140**

15in
38cm

Bead store

Necklace

20 g green size 11° seed beads

10 g green size 8° seed beads

Mix of size 11° seed beads in complementary colors

10 g size 10° triangles

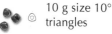
Flower and leaf beads

Clasp

Beading needle and thread

Bracelet

As the necklace but add more pink and red beads and extra embellishment beads.

8 Add a "bridge" of triangles between each spiral. Bring the needle out at the base of the first spiral. Add enough triangle beads to form a bridge. Thread through the top right corner at the back of the next spiral.

9 Pass down to the base of the next spiral and repeat. Continue along the row until every spiral is bridged.

The core of the necklace and bracelet

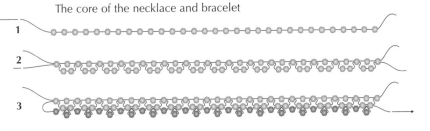

1

2

3

10 Attach embellishments to the bridges, or to any part of the spirals. Keep adding flowers and leaves until the section is packed. Leaves can be added to the lower edge so they fall on the neck.

TO COMPLETE NECKLACE

11 In this example, freeform peyote is added to make up the central section to the required length. However, a simpler option is to add a chain or rope (see page 82).

BRACELET

Thread the needle with about 60" (1.5 m) thread. Work as for the necklace, but add more pink beads, a splash of red beads, and some butterfly beads.

7in
19cm

hearts entwined

NECKLACE AND RING

This delicate peyote stitch spiral has a secret closure that makes it look seamless. A hint of pink in the heart accent beads added to the necklace brings the piece to life. The fairytale ring matches the necklace.

20in
51cm

Bead store

Necklace

◎ 15 g silver-gray size 11° seed beads

◎ 10 g pink size 11° seed beads

● 2 g pink size 15° seed beads

● 13 silver-gray/pink heart accent beads

Beading needle and thread

Ring

◎ 2 g silver-gray size 11° seed beads

◎ 2 g pink size 11° seed beads

⬡ 10 to 15 4mm fire-polished crystals

● 3 silver-gray/pink heart accent beads

18" (0.5 m) elastic beading thread

Clear nail polish

NECKLACE

1 Thread the needle, using about 60" (1.5 m) of thread. Pass one gray bead down to about 8" (20 cm) from the tail to form a stop bead.

2 Add 349 gray beads, using more or fewer to alter length. The example was worked to a gauge of eight beads to ½" (1.5 cm) but remember this may vary.

3 Work peyote stitch using gray beads, adding 2 beads where in standard peyote stitch you would add 1. Do not pull the thread too tightly, and let the beads fall as they will.
➤➤ **Peyote stitch, see page 114**

4 Work a third row using pink size 11° seed beads, placing a bead between each bead (including the pairs of beads) added on the previous row. The work will begin to spiral.

5 For the final row, place a pink bead between each of the pink beads in the third row.

6 Return to the stop bead and undo the thread loop using the point of the needle. String 14 gray beads, and pass back through the first bead to make a loop for the closure. Check its size by passing a heart bead through, then pass back into the work. Pass back through the loop to secure. Finish with a double knot.

7 Stand in front of a mirror and hold the necklace around your neck. Mark the position of the heart for fastening, using a pin. String 3 size 15° beads, a heart, and a size 15° bead. Pass back through the heart and 3 seed beads, then into the body of the work. Secure. Add more hearts as required.

RING

1 String 3 pink seed beads, a crystal, 3 pink beads, and another crystal onto the middle of the elastic thread. Pass the tail of the thread through the last crystal added. Pull ends firmly to form a square.

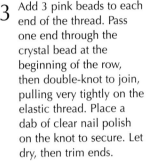

½in
1.25cm

2 Add 3 pink beads to one end of the thread, and 3 pink beads and a crystal to the other. Pass the end with the 3 seed beads through the crystal to form a second square. Repeat until there are enough squares to fit your finger.

3 Add 3 pink beads to each end of the thread. Pass one end through the crystal bead at the beginning of the row, then double-knot to join, pulling very tightly on the elastic thread. Place a dab of clear nail polish on the knot to secure. Let dry, then trim ends.

4 To attach the hearts, knot 40" (1 m) of thread to the top right corner of any square. String 2 gray beads, a heart, and 2 more gray beads. Pass up through the left crystal and add a gray bead. Pass down through the gray bead added on the first crossover, through the heart, then through the second gray bead. String another gray bead, and then pass back up through the right crystal again. Repeat for the last 2 hearts.

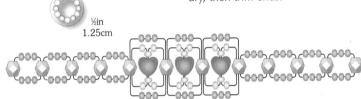

paradise island

NECKLACE AND RING

The centerpiece of this necklace is beautiful and needed limited decoration.
The base was worked in tubular peyote stitch. There are three sections to
the ring. Each can be worn alone, or wear all three for a stunning effect.

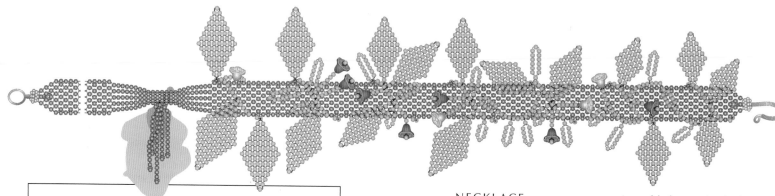

Bead store

Necklace

30 g size 11° seed
beads for necklace
rope

30 g size 11°
cylinder beads in
two or three colors

Orchid focal bead

Assorted bell-
shaped flower
accent beads

28" (70 cm) rats' tail for
core

Straw to bead around

Hook and loop closure

Beading needle and thread

Ring

5 g size 11° seed
beads

5 g size 11°
cylinder beads

2 bell-shaped
flower accent
beads

20" (0.5 m) fine elastic
beading cord

Beading needle and thread

NECKLACE

16in
40cm

1 Thread the needle using
60" (1.5 m) thread. String
15 size 11° seed beads,
leaving an 8" (20 cm)
tail. Tie in a circle using a
double knot.

2 Work in peyote stitch
until the tube is the
desired length. Allowing
for both the focal bead
and the necklace
fastening, work another
tube the same length.
➠ **Peyote stitch, see
page 114**

3 Pass the rats' tail through
one end of the fastening.
Double over, and move
the fastening to the
folded center.

4 Assemble by passing both
ends of the rats' tail
through one of the
beaded tubes, the hole in
the feature bead, the
second beaded tube and
the other end of the
fastener. Pull the rats' tail
up so only ¾" (2 cm)
shows. Double the ends
over and whipstitch to
the original length. Trim
close to work.

5 Work a spiral of beads
around the tubes by
bringing the needle out at
a bead on the top row.
String 5 or 6 cylinder
beads, hold them
diagonally on the tube,
and then take the thread
through the nearest seed
bead. Repeat, working
down the tube in a spiral
movement. Fill any gaps
as you return upward.

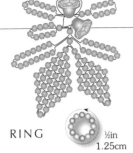

6 Using brick stitch and green cylinder beads, work diamond-shaped leaves in four sizes. Vary the number of beads in the center, where the shapes start. String leaves using 6, 7, 8, and 9 center beads. Work at least 4 in each size for each tube.
➤ **Brick stitch, see page 119**

7 Starting at the top of the vine, attach flowers and leaves. Add some small bead loops to add bulk and create texture. Bridge the gap between the two sections of tubing by stringing seed beads from one side of the tube to the other. This "bridge" will allow you to attach flowers and leaves around the orchid. Add strands of fringe that emerge from the orchid.
➤ **Adding a fringe, see page 137**

8 To finish the ends, work peyote stitch to reach the fastening. Work one or two more rows, decreasing so the beadwork sits snugly around the fastenings.

RING ½in 1.25cm

1 Cut three lengths of beading cord, each about 6" (15 cm) long. String enough seed beads to fit around your finger.

2 Double-knot the cord between the first and last beads added. Pull firmly to secure. Apply clear nail polish to strengthen the knot. Let dry, then trim ends close to knot.

3 Work two leaves as for the necklace. Work one with 6 beads across the center, and the other with 5 beads.

4 With the thread emerging from one end of the leaf, pass through a seed bead on the ring. Pass back down into the leaf.

5 Apply the second leaf to the next seed bead along in the same way. This provides a base for attaching the flowers. Add loops to give shape to the center. Make two more rings the same way.

snow princess

NECKLACE AND EARRINGS

Working with only one color is a wonderful exercise. Searching for different finishes and creating texture within the beadwork is a great challenge for any beader. This project was worked using plastic tubing. The earrings created to match the necklace are simple drops that hang directly from the findings.

NECKLACE

1 Cut a length of plastic tubing to fit neck, allowing space for clasp.

2 Double over 60" (1.5 m) of thread, pass ends through the eye of the needle. Pass through the eye on one side of the clasp. As you pull through, pass through the loop on the thread. Pull up to secure the fastening.

3 Pass right through the length of the tube, using a magnet if necessary to help to ease the needle through.

4 String enough size 8° beads to fill the tubing. Pull up so that the beads cover all the thread.

5 At the other side, pass through the second side of the clasp, and back down through the first 2 or 3 size 8° beads. Double-knot, and pass back up through these beads again. Cut off thread.

6 Work flat, rectangular pieces of even-count peyote in lots of different bead finishes to cover the tubing. Join them together over the tubing so they sit nice and tightly.
➤ **Peyote stitch, see page 114**

7 Create "bridges" between the peyote sections using size 11° seed beads to form a base for the floral accents. Attach flowers, leaves, and branch fringing as desired.
➤ **Branch fringing, see page 135**

Bead store

Necklace

 10 g size 8° seed beads

 Size 11° seed beads in assorted finishes

18" (0.5 m) plastic tubing

Clasp

Beading needle and thread

Earrings

 5 g size 11° seed beads

Accent beads

Earring findings

Beading needle and thread

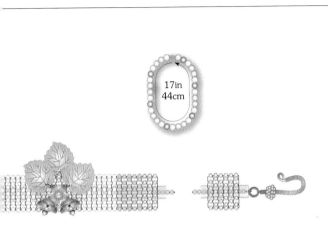

17in
44cm

1in
2.5cm

EARRINGS

1 Knot about 40″ (1 m) of thread onto an earring finding.

2 String seed beads to the length that you want the drop. Remember to allow for the accent bead at the base.

3 String the accent bead and a final seed bead. Pass back up the strand, skipping the final seed bead.

4 Loop the thread around the finding. Secure with a single knot. Work more strands of fringing. Add accent beads and fringing until the earrings are complete.

sea anemone

NECKLACE

This necklace makes a striking statement! It uses crystal, pearl, and opaque beads, plus bugles strung together for a spiky, textured look.

Bead store

 10 g size 6° seed beads

 10 g size 11° crystal seed beads

 10 g 6mm crystal bugles

 50 g bead mix

Clasp

Beading needle and thread

16in
41cm

1 Using doubled thread attach a toggle clasp.
➤ **Attaching a clasp, see page 140**

2 String 4 size 11° seed beads, and then string enough size 6° beads until the necklace is the required length. Finish with 4 size 11° beads. Pass through the other end of the clasp, then back through the size 11° beads and the first size 6° bead again.

3 Remove the thread from the needle, and double-knot between the first and second size 6° beads. Count the beads to divide the necklace into seven sections. If there are 140 beads, there will 20 beads in each section. If the number is not exactly divisible, incorporate an extra bead in one or two of the sections.

4 Using the bead mix and one of the threads, work fringing between each of the size 6° core beads. Work each strand using the same type of bead, with a seed bead at each end. Lengths depend on which section you are working. Follow the diagram as a guide. Vary the lengths to give a graduated effect.
➤ **Adding a fringe, see page 137**

5 Pass through the size 11° beads and the clasp. Turn. Pass through the size 11° beads and the first size 6° bead. Work a second row in the same way.

6 Turn as before and work a third row. Fasten off.
➤ **Starting and finishing threads, see page 138**

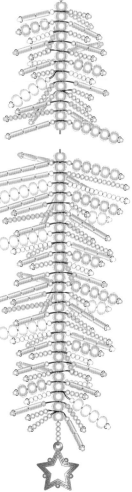

blue bead

NECKLACE

Here's a little magic trick in the making: Create a simple chain, or add a lovely focal bead as shown here. You'll work it up using tubular netting, but with three rather than the usual five accent color beads in the initial row.

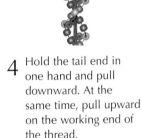

Bead store

 15 g size 11° seed beads (main color)

 10 g size 11° seed beads (accent color)

1 focal bead

Clasp

20" (50 cm) gimp cord/rats' tail

Beading needle and thread

15in
38cm

1 Using 60" (1.5 m) of thread, and leaving a 6" (15 cm) tail end, string 1 accent color seed bead, 2 main color beads, 1 accent color, 2 main color, 1 accent color, then 2 more main color beads. Pass the needle through the first bead again to form a circle.
➤ **Tubular netting, see page 124**

2 Add 2 main, 1 accent color, and another 2 main color beads. Pass the needle through the second accent color bead along on the first circle. Keep the work flat until the next few beads are in place.

3 Add 2 main, 1 accent, and another 2 main color beads. Pass the needle through the second accent color bead (the center bead of the group just added) again.

4 Hold the tail end in one hand and pull downward. At the same time, pull upward on the working end of the thread.

5 Continue to add sets of beads in the same way.

6 Work two separate lengths, each half the length of your necklace, remembering to include the focal bead and clasp.

7 Pass the rats' tail through the sections of necklace, centering the focal bead. Pass through one section of the clasp, and sew the end in place. Cut off any excess, pulling the netting over the stitches to hide them. Repeat on the other side.
➤ **Attaching a clasp, see page 140**

daisy chain
NECKLACE

You'll love the simple charm and elegance of this piece. Inspired by the daisy chains made by children, it looks best when worn as a short necklace.

Bead store

 10 g size 11° seed beads

 12 size 15° seed beads

 12 bell-shaped flower beads with a vertical hole through the center

 12 4mm crystals

Clasp

Beading needle and thread

REPEAT

15in
38cm

1 Thread the needle using about 36″ (90 cm) of beading thread. String 10 size 11° seed beads and position just over halfway from the other end of the thread.
➤ **Simple stringing, see page 132**

2 Add a flower bead, a crystal, and a size 15° bead. Pass the thread back through the crystal and flower beads, making sure it is pulled up so no excess shows.

3 String 10 more size 11° seed beads, a flower, a crystal, and a size 15° bead. Repeat as before until all the flower beads have been used.

4 Finish by adding size 11° seed beads to each end until the required length is reached. Attach the clasp.
➤ **Attaching a clasp, see page 140**

blue drop flower
NECKLACE

This stylish necklace combines the sweet, simple lines of bellflowers, and flame-blue seed beads. You can adjust the length and choose the way in which the necklace is fastened around your neck.

1 Thread the needle with about 60" (1.5 m) of thread. String 1 size 11° seed bead, and take it to within 4" (10 cm) of the end of the thread. Take the needle back through the bead to form a stop bead.

2 String 6 more seed beads,* 1 flower bead, 4 seed beads, 1 flower bead. Repeat from * until there are 5 flowers at one end of the thread. Thread a length of seed beads for the body of the necklace.

3 Thread on 6 seed beads. Working as before, add more flower beads interspersed with seed beads. For the example, six more flowers were added but this can be varied.

4 After the last flower bead, string 6 more seed beads. Skipping the last seed bead added, take the thread back through the entire length of the necklace.

5 At the end of the necklace, add 5 seed beads to make a small tassel.

6 Work the needle back through the length of the necklace. Come back through the beads as before. Add a tassel at the other end.

20in
51cm

REPEAT

Bead store

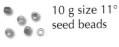
10 g size 11° seed beads

11 bellflower accent beads

Beading needle and thread

purple rainforest
NECKLACE

For this necklace, less is definitely more. The beautiful bead at its center only needed a simple, elegant mount.

Bead store

- 30 g size 15° seed beads
- 2 size 6° seed beads

Focal bead

4 cylinder beads

Clasp

Drinking straw (to help form the tube)

Beading needle and thread

1 Cut the straw lengthwise all the way down. Thread the needle with about 40" (1 m) of thread. String 22 size 15° seed beads, and move them down to within 4" (10 cm) of the thread end.

2 Pass through all 22 beads again to form a circle. Slip the circle over the top of the straw, and double-knot the two threads.

3 Work tubular peyote stitch. Repeat Steps 1 to 3 to work a second length.
➤➤ **Peyote stitch, see page 114**

4 To link the necklace, thread the needle with about 60" (1.5 m) of thread. Attach one end to one side of the clasp, leaving a 4" (10 cm) tail. String a size 6° bead, a cylinder bead, and one of the peyote stitch tubes.

5 String a cylinder bead, the focal bead, a cylinder bead, the second peyote stitch tube, the final cylinder, and a size 6° bead. Pass through the other side of the clasp.

6 Strengthen the necklace by passing backward and forward from the clasp to the peyote stitch tube. Strengthen the area around the focal bead by passing a thread from the end of the peyote tube by the focal bead through to the other opposite tube. Repeat several times.

15in
39cm

herringbone rope
NECKLACE

Here's a simple but alluring rope necklace. You can work it using a combination of matte and shiny triangle beads, which complement each other well and create a fun texture.

Bead store

 ⚠ 10 g matte size 11° triangles

⚠ 10 g shiny size 10° triangles

Clasp

Beading needle and thread

15in
39cm

1 Thread the needle with about 60" (1.5 m) of thread, leaving an 8" (20 cm) tail for attaching the clasp. Begin with 4 matte triangles in a brick stitch ladder, and work tubular herringbone stitch.
➤ **Ladder stitch, see page 118**
➤ **Herringbone stitch, see page 126**

2 Work three rows, including the brick stitch ladder start. Choose the combination for the triangles, or work this way: twenty rows shiny, five rows matte, fifteen rows shiny, ten rows matte, ten rows shiny, fifteen rows matte and five rows shiny. For a longer necklace, add any combination of extra triangles here.

3 Repeat the pattern in reverse for the other side of the necklace.

4 Attach the clasp.
➤ **Attaching a clasp, see page 140**

paua shell

NECKLACE AND BRACELET

These beautiful, iridescent shells contain many different colors. In this design, seed beads and chips of semi precious stone in complementary tones highlight the blues and greens. This bracelet has three large shells in the center, and becomes more delicate toward the ends.

17in
43cm

Bead store

Necklace

 20 g size 11° seed beads, mixed

5 g size 11° blue seed beads

Large piece of drilled paua shell

Small pieces of drilled paua shell

Semiprecious stone chips

6mm round bead (for clasp)

Beading needle and thread

Bracelet

 10 g size 6° seed beads

 20 g size 11° mixed seed beads

 5 g size 15° seed beads in the same colors

Paua shells in assorted sizes and semiprecious stone chips

 4mm round matte pearl beads

 6mm round matte pearl beads

Beading needle and thread

NECKLACE

1 Thread the needle with about 60" (1.5 m) of thread. String 3 size 15° seed beads, the large piece of shell, and 3 more size 15° beads. Move to the center of the thread.

2 Bring the ends of the thread together, and pass both through the beading needle. String a size 11° seed bead, a piece of shell, a stone chip, 5 seed beads, a piece of shell, a stone chip, 5 seed beads, a piece of shell, a stone chip, and a piece of shell.
➤ **Simple stringing, see page 132**

3 Remove a strand of thread from the needle, and use the other to work one side of the necklace. * String 25 seed beads, a stone chip, a piece of shell, and another stone chip. Repeat from *.

4 To make the first half of the clasp, add the 6mm bead and 1 seed bead. Pass back through the 6mm bead, then through the necklace to give added strength. Double-knot to finish.
➤ **Attaching a clasp, see page 140**

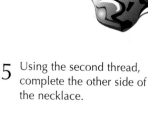

5 Using the second thread, complete the other side of the necklace.

6 To make the second half of the clasp, string seed beads to form a loop that fits snugly over the 6mm bead. Pass back through the first bead, and then back down into the body of the necklace. Pass through the beads in the loop again.

BRACELET

1 Thread the needle with about 60" (1.5 m) of thread. Place 1 size 11° seed bead in the center. Place the ends of the thread together and pass both through the eye of the needle.

7in
18cm

2 Add 1 6mm bead for the first part of the clasp. String 4 size 11° seed beads, then size 6° seed beads to the length required for the bracelet. Add 4 more size 11° beads. Using size 11° seed beads, form a loop as in Step 6 of the necklace.

3 Thread back down through the first size 6° seed bead.

4 Letting your imagination run free, embellish the bracelet. In the example, this was added using fringe and branch fringe. Two holes were drilled in the larger shells so they could be strung with beads. Branch fringe was added on the second pass across the work.
▶ Adding a fringe, see page 137
▶ Drilling, see page 134

pink mussel

NECKLACE

These gorgeous pink mussel shells inspired this necklace.

Bead store

 Pink mussel shells in various sizes

 8mm pearl bead

 10 g size 11° seed beads in each of 3 colors

Clasp

Beading needle and thread

1 Thread about 60" (1.5 m) of thread through a large mussel shell until it sits in the center. String 2 seed beads (back of the shell), and 3 seed beads (front) to cover and strengthen the threads.

2 Place the ends of the thread together, and take both through the eye of the needle. String 1 pearl bead, and 1 seed bead. Remove one of the threads from the needle. Use the other to work one side of the necklace.

3 String 20 seed beads in one of the colors, and a mussel shell. Repeat until work is long enough. Take the needle through one side of the clasp and turn.

4 Work another string using 20 seed beads in the second color between each mussel shell.

5 Work down to the focal shell. Take the needle back through the beads again around this "drop" section. Turn to work the last row of this side.

6 Work a final string, using 20 beads in the third color between each shell. Take the string around the other two if you want a woven effect. Finish off.
➤➤ **Starting and finishing threads, see page 138**

7 Using the second thread, work the other side of the necklace in the same way.

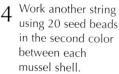

18in
46cm

Starting and finishing threads, see page 138

freshwater pearl
NECKLACE

The irregularities in these slices of freshwater pearl attract the light, and highlight their natural beauty.

Bead store

15 g size 11° seed beads

16 to 20 freshwater pearl slices

Drilled mother-of-pearl disc

Clasp

Beading needle and thread

1 Thread the needle with about 60" (1.5 m) of thread. Pass through the eye on one side of the clasp. Double-knot the thread onto the clasp, leaving a 4" (10 cm) tail.

2 Thread on 15 seed beads, then a pearl slice. Repeat until the work is the required length.
➤ **Simple stringing, see page 132**

3 Add 17 seed beads, the disc, and then 17 more beads. The 2 "extra" beads here cover the disc on either side of the hole. Pass the needle back through the last pearl slice.

4 Work toward the clasp end, adding 15 beads between each pearl slice.

5 Work backward and forward, adding strands of beads to the necklace sections.

6 Complete the other side of the necklace in the same way, reversing the design of the first side. Fasten off the ends of the thread. Trim close to work.
➤ **Starting and finishing threads, see page 138**

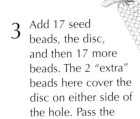

15in
38cm

enchanted forest
— NECKLACE —

The inspiration behind this project was a fantastic piece of embossed, frosted glass, but a slice of gemstone or agate would look great.

Bead store

 Size 11° seed beads in four or five complementary colors

 30 g size 11° seed beads for rope

 5 g size 15° seed beads

Accent beads for embellishment

Piece of embossed glass, cabochon, or an agate slice

Clasp

Beading needle and thread

1 Thread the needle with about 60" (1.5 m) of thread. String an even number of size 11° seed beads, and knot into a circle, about 20 percent smaller than the outer edge of the form you want to enclose.

2 Work in rounds of fairly loose peyote stitch. Continue until two or three rows of peyote stitch are visible when you place the form on top of the work.
▶ **Peyote stitch, see page 114**

3 Hold the beadwork and form tightly between your fingers, and continue in peyote stitch.

4 Continue, decreasing as necessary to achieve a clean finish. Do this by passing the thread across to close the gap between two beads on the previous row, instead of adding a bead.

9in
23cm

5 Add leaves, flowers, fringe, and extra seed beads to enhance the piece.

6 Work a small, flat rectangle of herringbone stitch. Loop over and attach to back of pendant as a hanging point.
▶ **Herringbone stitch, see page 126**

7 Add a rope worked in size 11° seed beads using tubular herringbone stitch, from a ladder stitch base of eight beads.
▶ **Ladder stitch starting method, see page 126**

olive and amethyst

NECKLACE

This simple, two-row necklace uses bellflower accent beads as innovative settings for the stunning olive pearls. The top row sits at the base of the neck and the second just below.

Bead store

 10 g size 11° seed beads

 60 to 80 6mm pearl beads

 48 to 68 bellflower beads

 42 to 62 shallow bellflower beads

Clasp

Beading needle and thread

16in
41cm

1 Thread the needle with about 60" (1.5 m) of thread. Attach one end to the clasp by knotting.
➤ **Attaching a clasp, see page 140**

2 String the top row using 12 seed beads, * 1 bellflower bead, 1 pearl, 1 bellflower bead, 1 seed bead. Repeat from * until the necklace is the length required. String 12 more seed beads.
➤ **Simple stringing, see page 132**

3 Remove the other side of the clasp. Pass the needle through the eye, and then through the 12 seed beads and the first flower bead.

4 Double-knot between the flower bead and pearl. Pass through a few more beads. Double-knot again.

5 Thread the needle as in Step 1. Attach to one end of the clasp. String 20 seed beads, * 1 shallow bellflower, 1 pearl, 1 shallow bellflower, 2 seed beads. Repeat from * to end (eight to ten sets of pearls and flowers).

6 For the center section, string three 5-pearl blocks, with two sets of flowers and pearls between. Repeat as before for second side.

7 Secure to the other side of the clasp. Finish in the usual way.
➤ **Starting and finishing threads, see page 138**

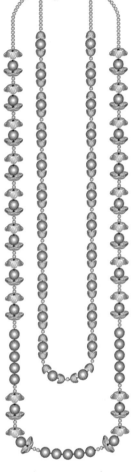

coffee and cream
NECKLACE AND EARRINGS

Crystals and pearls create a stunning combination when light reflects the silky-smooth finish of the pearls against the sparkle of the crystals. To give the set an elegant, uncluttered look, the earrings echo the initial stringing pattern of the necklace.

NECKLACE

1 Thread the needle with 60" (1.5 m) of thread. Attach one end to the clasp.
➤ **Attaching a clasp, see page 140**

2 For the first row, string a size 11° seed bead,* a size 6° bead, a 6mm crystal, a size 6° bead, a 6mm pearl, an 8mm pearl, a 6mm pearl, repeat from * until the necklace is the required length. Finish with a size 11° seed bead.

3 Remove the other side of the clasp. Pass the needle through the eye of the clasp, then through the first 5 beads strung, emerging on the far side of the first 6mm pearl.

4 To make the beaded fringe, string 2 size 11° seed beads, one 4mm crystal, and 1 size 11° bead. Pass the needle back through the crystal and the seed beads, then through the next bead, an 8mm pearl.
➤ **Adding a fringe, see page 137**

5 Add another strand of fringe, and then pass the needle through the 6mm pearl on the other side of the 8mm pearl. Continue in this way, adding a strand of fringe on either side of each 8mm pearl.

6 At the end of the row, turn by threading through the clasp. Work a second row of fringing between the same beads, but using 1 size 11° seed bead, one 4mm crystal, and 1 size 11° seed bead.

7 Repeat Step 6, working up and down the initial string, until there are five strands of fringe on either side of each 8mm pearl. Make sure that the strand of fringe with 2 seed beads at its base is in the center of each group, as it gives a neat, graduated look.

Bead store

Necklace

 10 g size 11° seed beads

 10 g size 6° seed beads

 15 to 20 8mm pearl beads

 30 to 35 6mm pearl beads

 16 to 20 6mm crystals

 135 to 150 4mm crystals

Clasp

Earring findings

Beading thread and needle

Earrings
As the necklace but adapt amounts to suit the length of the earrings.

17in 44cm

EARRINGS

1 Thread the needle with about 40" (1 m) of thread. Attach one end to the earring finding, leaving a tail about 4" (10 cm) long.

2 String a size 11° seed bead, a size 6° seed bead, an 8mm pearl, a size 6° bead, a 6mm pearl, a size 6° bead, a 6mm crystal, a size 6° bead, a size 11° bead, a 4mm crystal, a size 11° bead, a 4mm crystal, and 3 size 11° beads.

2in
5cm

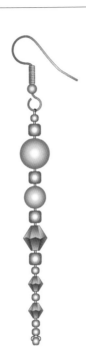

3 Skip the last seed bead, and pass the needle back through the next 2 beads on the initial string. Tie a double knot between them and weave through 2 or 3 beads. Trim close to work.

4 Thread the needle on the other end of the thread. Complete as in Step 3.

Victorian collar

NECKLACE

This is the most classic of all classic necklaces. It lies beautifully on the neck, and is a must in any jewelry collection.

Bead store

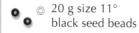 20 g size 11° black seed beads

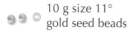 10 g size 11° gold seed beads

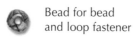 Bead for bead and loop fastener

Clasp

Beading needle and thread

14in
35cm

1 Thread beading needle with about 60" (1.5 m) of thread. Leave a 12" (30 cm) tail and thread on 1 gold bead to create a stop bead.

2 String 4 black, 1 gold, 4 black, 1 gold, 5 black, and 4 gold beads. Pass through the first of the 4 gold beads to make a small diamond.

3 String 5 black, 1 gold, and 4 black beads. Pass through the second gold bead of Row 1, to form a diamond with 1 gold bead at each point.

4 String 4 black, 1 gold, 4 black, 1 gold, and 4 black beads. Pass through the gold bead on the right of the first diamond.

5 String 5 black and 4 gold beads. Pass through the first of the 4 gold beads to form another diamond. String 5 more black, 1 gold, and 4 black beads. Pass through the center side bead of the last diamond made. Repeat until work measures 8" (20 cm).

6 To gather the netting, measure enough thread, and add 16" (40 cm). Remove loop around stop bead. Leaving an 8" (20 cm) tail, make a knot against the first gold bead.

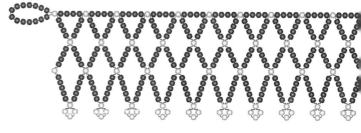

7 Pass through the first gold bead on the top row. String 4 black beads. *Pass through the second gold bead. String 4 more beads. Repeat from *, work a further section, then gather.

8 Work to the length required. Add a bead and loop fastener.
➤ **Bead and loop fasteners, see page 141**

pink diamonds
NECKLACE

The key elements of this piece are delicacy and femininity.
You could use the rosette centerpiece for many different
types of jewelry pieces.

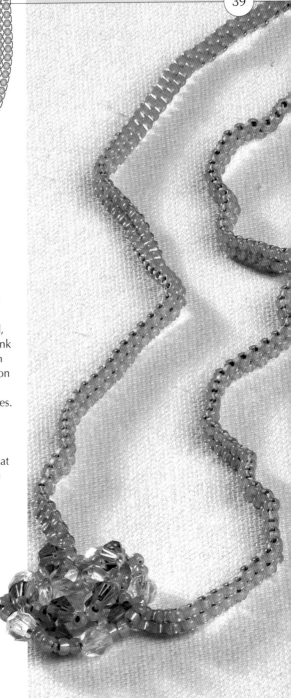

Bead store

 10 g pink size 11° seed beads

 5 g crystal size 11° seed beads

10 4mm pink crystals

10 4mm fire-polished crystals

Clasp

Beading needle and thread

15in
38cm

1 Thread the needle with about 40" (1 m) of thread leaving an 8" (20 cm) tail. String a seed bead, then a fire-polished crystal. Repeat four times. Pass the tail through the beads. Secure in a circle using a double knot.

2 Pass the needle through the next pink seed bead along. String a pink seed bead, a pink crystal, and a pink seed bead. Pass through the next seed bead of the first row. String 4 more pink crystals to complete the second row.

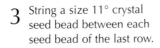

3 String a size 11° crystal seed bead between each seed bead of the last row.

4 Bring the needle out of the next pink crystal along. String a pink seed bead, a fire-polished crystal, and a pink seed bead. Pass through the next pink crystal. Repeat to end.

5 Pass through a seed bead at the side of a crystal bead. String 3 pink seed beads, and then pass through the next pink seed bead. String 3 more pink seed beads. Repeat to the row end.

6 Pass through one of the first row seed beads. String 1 pink seed bead, 1 pink crystal, and 1 pink seed bead. Pass through to the next seed bead, on the other side of the crystal. Repeat four times.

7 Work peyote stitch, 2 beads wide, beginning at 1 of the beads from the sets of 3 added in Step 5. Work a length from both sides to form the necklace. Add a clasp.
➤➤ **Peyote stitch, see page 114**
➤➤ **Adding a clasp, see page 140**

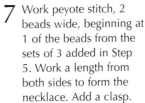

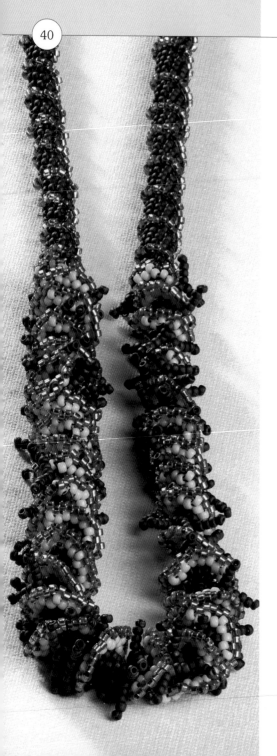

sea urchin
NECKLACE

This longer necklace combines both tubular and spiral peyote stitch. The focal point is the pink beads, which spiral up the peyote tubes to bring the whole piece together.

25in 64cm

Bead store

○ 40 g charcoal gray size 11° seed beads

○ 15 g pink size 11° seed beads

○ 10 g green size 11° seed beads

Clasp

Beading needle and thread

1 Thread needle with 60" (1.5 m) thread, and make a stop bead with 1 charcoal bead. String on a further 199 beads.

2 Using charcoal beads, work the first three rows as for *Hearts Entwined* (page 18, Steps 2 to 4). On the second row, string 2 beads over every other bead. On the third, string 1 bead between each bead. Pull as you work to encourage the spiral.

3 On Row 4, string 2 green beads between each bead added on the previous row.

4 On Rows 5 and 6, string 1 pink bead between each bead on the previous row, to mark the edge of the spiral with a pink outline.

5 Pass back along the core beads. Using charcoal beads, work branch fringing in the small gaps between each spiral.
➤ **Branch fringing, see page 135**

6 Work two tubular peyote stitch tubes in the required width. Attach to the spiral, "wrapping" one end to hide the joins. Stitch in place. Repeat for the opposite side.
➤ **Peyote stitch, see page 114**

7 Bring the needle out from the last pink bead at the end of the spiral attached to the tube. String 5 or 6 pink beads, and hold them around the tube in an upward spiral direction. Take the needle through the nearest corresponding bead on the peyote tube, and string the next 5 or 6 pink beads. Repeat to the top end of the tube.

8 Work a spiral of beads around the tube as in *Paradise Island*, (page 20, Step 5). Add a clasp.
➤ **Attaching a clasp, see page 140**

licorice allsorts

BRACELET

The base of this fun bracelet is clear plastic tubing. The examples show a few ideas for the "allsorts," but the possibilities are endless. They may be made separately, but it is easier to work around a solid base.

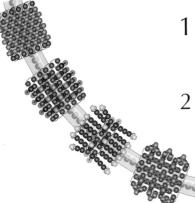

1 Follow Steps 1 to 5 of *Snow Princess* (page 22), to form the base.

2 Attach the clasp.
➤ **Attaching a clasp, see page 140**

9in
23cm

5 For the conical end beads, make a peyote stitch rectangle 4 beads wide. Attach to the tubing so it sits a little way from the edge. At the end nearest the edge, work a row of brick stitch using the loops from the peyote stitch. Work three more rows of brick stitch, decreasing once or twice on each row, so the beadwork draws in. To decrease, skip a loop and take the needle through the next loop, 1 bead along. Pull as you work, to close the gap.
➤ **Brick stitch, see page 119**

Bead store

 10 g black size 8° beads

 20 g black size 11° seed beads

 10 g seed beads in a mix of bright colors

20" (0.5 m) plastic tubing (available from aquatic stores)

Clasp

Beading needle and thread

3 Start each "allsort" by making with a strip of peyote stitch. This can range from 4 beads across to 8 or 10. Secure to the tubing by zipping the two sides together, threading from side to side. Embellish each allsort strip with bright beads.
➤ **Peyote stitch, see page 114**

4 Work a selection of "allsorts." Leave space between the "allsorts" so that the size 8° beads can be seen.

blue dagger drop
NECKLACE

Bead store

14 blue size 11°
seed beads

3 large blue
dagger beads

10 small blue
flower beads

Silver crimp
beads

Clasp

40" (1 m) plastic-coated
beading wire

Cutting and crimping
pliers

14in
35cm

This delicate look can be achieved in minutes using a few simple accent beads plus crimp beads and wire.

1 Lay the wire flat on a beading mat. String 1 crimp, 1 seed bead, 1 flower, 1 dagger bead, 1 flower, 1 seed bead, and 1 crimp. Center the beads. Crimp both crimp beads.
➤ **Crimping, see page 134**

2 Working on one side, leave a ⅓" (7 mm) gap. String 1 crimp, 1 seed bead, 1 flower, 1 seed bead, and 1 crimp. Crimp both crimp beads in place.

3 Add two more sets of beads, the next using a dagger bead and seed beads and the final set with just a flower and seed beads. Crimp both in place.

4 Repeat Steps 2 and 3 for the other side of the necklace.

5 Add the clasp using crimp beads. Check the length of the necklace before fixing in place.
➤ **Attaching a clasp, see page 140**

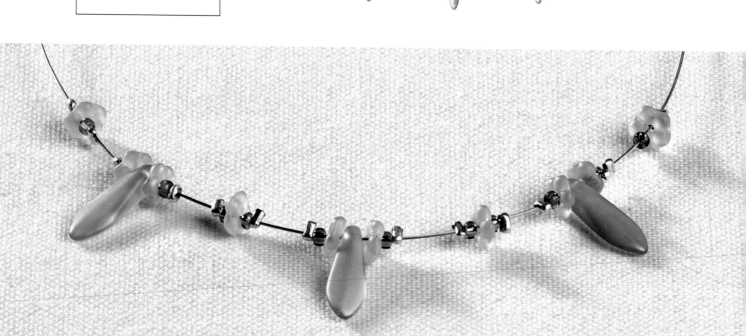

devotion
NECKLACE

This Venetian glass bead just needed simple stringing to highlight its radiant beauty. Topaz-colored beads and red cord echo its gold and red tones.

Bead store

  10 g matte topaz size 6° seed beads

2 faceted 8mm beads

Heart focal bead

2 flat leather crimp beads

40" (1 m) red waxed cotton cord

Clasp

Beading needle and thread

16in
41cm

1 Lay the cord on a beading mat. String 2 topaz beads and pass them down to the center.

2 String the heart bead and pass it down so it sits on top of the topaz beads.

3 String a faceted bead from each end of the cord to sit on either side of the topaz beads. This "locks" the heart in place in the center of the necklace.

4 String topaz beads on each end of the cord to the required length.

5 Place a flat leather crimp at the base of the last bead added. Fold the sides over to secure the cord. Repeat for the other side of the necklace.
➤➤ **Working with metal findings, see page 134**

6 Attach the clasp. Trim ends.
➤➤ **Attaching a clasp, see page 140**

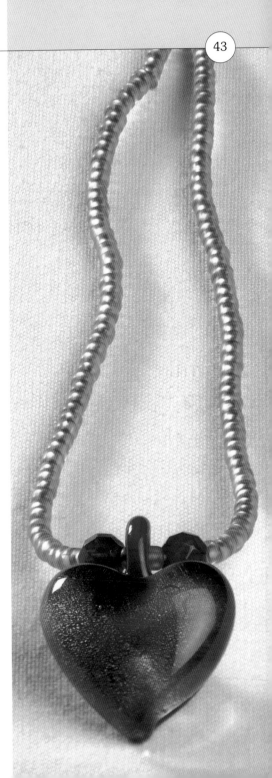

floating pinks

NECKLACE

This necklace is simple and quick to make, yet very pretty. Tiger tail looks so delicate that a lovely effect can be achieved by adding very little. To make it easier to place the knot cups and lobster clasp, use a longer section of tiger tail than is actually needed.

Bead store

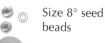

17in 44cm

◎ Size 8° seed beads

Focal beads

○ Minicrimp beads

Lobster clasp and jump ring

2 knot cups

16" (40 cm) 0.18 diameter tiger tail

Cutting, round nose, flat nose, and crimping pliers

1 Working flat and using the tiger tail, string 1 crimp bead, 1 seed bead, 1 focal bead, a seed bead and a crimp bead.

2 Using the crimping pliers, clamp down on the crimp bead nearest the end of the tiger tail. Make sure there are no gaps, and then clamp down on the crimp bead at the other end.

3 Leaving a gap between each, add groups of beads. Clamp down the crimp beads on either side of each group to hold them in place. Complete the necklace, ready to attach the clasp.

➤ **Crimping, see page 134**

4 Pass one end of the tiger tail between the hinge of the knot cup. Loop the tiger tail around and pass the end back through the hinge.

5 Using flat-nose pliers, clamp down on the knot cup covering the loop. Cut off any excess tiger tail. Attach a knot cup to the other end in the same way.

6 Attach the jump ring to one side and the lobster clasp to the other. Use the round-nose pliers to close the loop.

➤ **Attaching a clasp, see page 140**

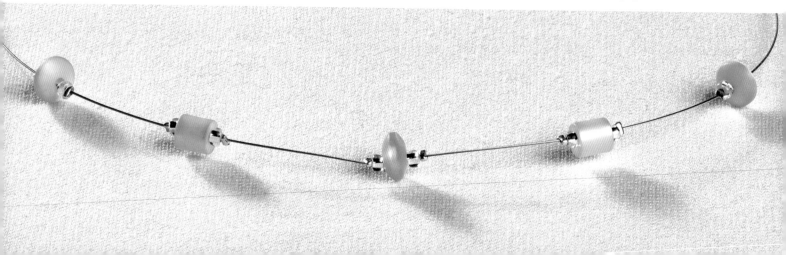

layered spiral
NECKLACE

Three focal beads inspired this piece. Alone, they were unremarkable, but the design strengthened their effect. Lengths of spiral peyote were made separately, and then put together with the beads.

Bead store

 20 g size 11° seed beads (main color)

 10 g size 11° seed beads (accent color)

Focal beads

Clasp

Beading needle and thread

17in
44cm

1 For the shorter necklace row, use about 40" (1 m) of thread. Take a main color seed bead to within 6" (15 cm) of the tail end. Pass back to make a stop bead. Add 130 more main color seed beads.

2 Work peyote stitch back along the first row, adding 2 beads where in standard peyote stitch 1 would be added. Do not pull too tightly.
➤ **Peyote stitch, see page 114**

3 Work a third row in peyote stitch, but adding 1 bead between each of the beads on Row 2. A bead should be placed between every pair of beads. On this row, pull as you work. The rope should begin to spiral.

4 Work another section in exactly the same way.

5 For the longer necklace row, work three lengths in the same way, each with 100 seed beads.

6 Assemble the necklace using beading thread. Place 1 focal bead in the center of the top row, and 2 focal beads between bottom row sections.
➤ **Starting and finishing threads, see page 138**

7 Attach a clasp.
➤ **Adding a clasp, see page 140**

Serengeti sunrise
NECKLACE

String wooden beads in striking animal prints using a simple, relaxed technique. Cut the ends just before you begin for ease of threading.

Bead store

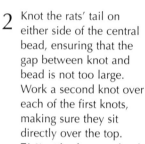

Animal print beads in assorted sizes

Flat leather crimp findings

Jump rings

Clasp

40" (1 m) copper-colored rats' tail

Flat-nose pliers

18in
45cm

1 Lay the rats' tail flat. Pass a large animal print bead down so it sits at the center of the necklace.

2 Knot the rats' tail on either side of the central bead, ensuring that the gap between knot and bead is not too large. Work a second knot over each of the first knots, making sure they sit directly over the top.
➤ **Knotting between beads, see page 139**

3 String beads from both ends of the necklace in the same sequence. Make a double knot between each large bead. A single knot will be adequate between smaller beads.
➤ **Simple stringing, see page 132**

4 Continue stringing beads to the end, or leave a length of rats' tail to show off its color.

5 Position the flat leather crimps and clamp into place. Trim ends.
➤ **Working with metal findings, see page 134**

6 Attach the clasp.
➤ **Attaching a clasp, see page 140**

African safari
NECKLACE

Faux tortoiseshell, amber, and glass beads are really effective in this necklace. The two-bar clasp helps it to sit well. A necklace bust would be useful for positioning the strings.

Bead store

Glass beads in assorted sizes and shapes

Crimp beads

Clasp

60″ (1.5 m) plastic-coated beading wire

Crimping pliers

16in
41cm

1 Experiment with different combinations of beads for the upper row, using a beading board.
➤ **Simple stringing, see page 132**

2 Cut the length of wire in half and lay one piece flat on a beading mat.

3 Pass a crimp bead down the wire. String the chosen combination of beads. Add a second crimp bead.

4 Make sure the row is centered as far as possible. Using crimping pliers, crimp both crimp beads in place.

5 String 2 crimp beads on one end of the wire and pass through the upper eye on one side of the clasp. Move both crimps up toward the clasp end of the necklace.

6 Pass the end of the wire down through the crimp beads, and push them up until you can see only a small loop of wire coming from the clasp. Make sure the necklace is the right length, then crimp the crimp beads in place.

7 Fasten the other end of the wire to the clasp. Trim any excess as close to the crimps as possible. Plan the second string and complete in the same way.

8 Arrange the second string to hang just below the first, using a necklace bust if possible. Crimp the crimp beads in place on both sides. Trim wire.

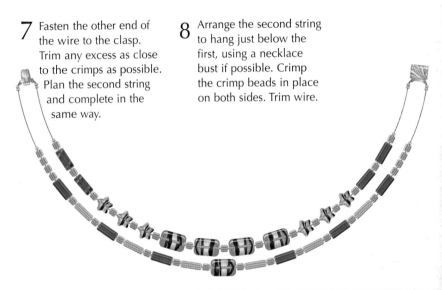

fandango
NECKLACE

This simple and flattering necklace can be made in an evening. It fastens by doubling over and passing the fringed end through the loop—so make sure it is long enough.

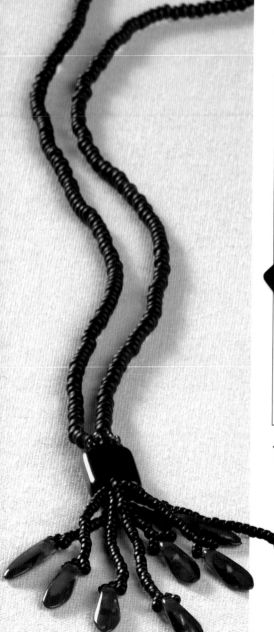

Bead store

- 15 g size 8° seed beads

- 5 g size 11° seed beads

- 8 to 10 size 11° seed beads (color to match dagger beads)

- Large accent bead

- 8 large dagger beads

Beading needle and thread

1 Thread the needle with 60" (1.5 m) of thread. String size 8° seed beads for the main loop, adding a few extra. Double over, and pass both ends of the thread through a size 8° bead. Pass through the large accent bead. Double-knot together.

2 Thread the needle with one of the threads. Pass it back up through the large accent bead and leave.

3 Thread up the other thread. String 30 size 11° beads, a dagger bead, and 2 more size 11° beads. Pass up through the third bead before the dagger. Pass through the remaining beads, then the accent bead. Knot around the top, and then pass back down through the accent bead.

4 Work more strands of fringe as in Step 3. Work two strands using 25 seed beads before the dagger bead, two using 20 beads before the dagger, two using 15 beads before the dagger, and one using 10 beads before the dagger.

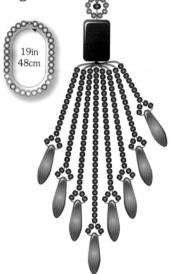

19in 48cm

5 Take the thread back up through the accent bead. Using thread that matches the dagger beads, add 8 to 10 size 11° beads. Pass thread around the last size 8° bead to form a circle. Pass back through the first bead and double-knot in place. Pass through 2 further beads. Cut off.

6 Return to the thread left in Step 2. Pass through the main core of the necklace again and finish.

❯❯ Starting and finishing threads, see page 138

sea creature
NECKLACE

This necklace combines a simple spiral rope and spiky tentacles with shocking-pink tips. Add as much or as little embellishment as you like. Practice the spiral rope first (see page 84), using two colors so it is easier to see the technique.

Bead store

 30 g size 11° cylinder beads

 10 g size 11° seed beads

Small, round accent bead for clasp

Beading needle and thread

15in
39cm

1 Thread the needle using about 40" (1 m) of thread. String 7 cylinder beads. Pass through the first 4 beads again.

2 String 4 cylinder beads,* let them drop down to the initial circle.

3 Pass through the second, third, and fourth bead on the original circle, and then the first of the 4 beads just added.

4 String 4 cylinder beads. Repeat from * until the necklace is the length required.

5 Add the "tentacles" to the sets of 3 beads that spiral around the inner core of the rope. Bring the needle out of one of the sets of beads. String seed beads until the tentacle is the required length. Add 1 pink bead. Skip this bead, and take the needle back through the tentacle and into the main body of the necklace again.

6 Add as many tentacles as you wish. Varying their length is also very effective.

graphite stone

— NECKLACE —

Framed in circular peyote stitch, the crystals glint and peek from the agate slice. Minimal beading in complementary colors lets its beauty shine through.

Bead store

 Assorted size 11° seed beads

 Assorted larger beads in colors to complement agate

 Silver crimp beads

Agate slice

Clasp

2 knot cups

Nylon-coated jewelry wire

Beading needle and thread

1 Cover the edge of the slice with flat, circular peyote stitch, increasing and decreasing as necessary for a snug fit.
➤ **Flat circular peyote stitch, see page 115**

2 Cut a length of wire, allowing 8″ (20 cm) extra. String enough seed beads to circle the hole in the slice. Pass the wire back through the first bead to form a loop.

3 String a crimp bead and pass down to the top of the loop. Clamp in place to secure the bead loop.

4 String the first set of beads in your chosen order. Clamp a crimp bead in place.

5 Part the two wires and bead separately until the required length is reached.

6 Place a knot cup on both sides of the wire. Knot the wire where you wish the crimp bead to sit, and slide the knot cup into position. Trim any excess wire. Clamp the knot cup in place.

7 Using round-nose pliers, place the clasp into the rounded loops of the knot cup. Bend into position.

blacklip shell
NECKLACE

A shell like this is so inspirational, you'll dream up plenty of design ideas. Here's just one. Remember, though, that when you find a really special focal bead, keep the rest of the beads simple.

Bead store

 3 disk beads

 Gold crimp beads

Marble-effect beads in assorted shapes

Focal bead

Gold nylon-coated wire

2 knot cups

Crimping pliers

Round-nose pliers

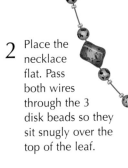

19in
48cm

1 Cut a length of wire for the necklace, allowing 8″ (20 cm) extra for finishing. Pass both ends through the hole at the front of the leaf to form a loop. Pass the ends back through the loop and pull up firmly to tighten it around the top of the leaf.

2 Place the necklace flat. Pass both wires through the 3 disk beads so they sit snugly over the top of the leaf.

3 Add a crimp bead to each wire to separate the two sides of the necklace. String beads in any combination you like, separating each group with a crimp bead.
➤ **Simple stringing, see page 132**

4 Crimp the crimp beads using crimping pliers. Repeat until the necklace is the length required.

5 Hold the necklace up to check the position of the fastening. Place it flat, then pass the end through the hinged end of a knot cup. Knot the wire.

6 Move the knot cup over the knot. Trim any excess and clamp the knot cup into place. Repeat for the other side.

7 Fit a clasp to the looped end of the knot cup using round-nose pliers.

Springtime blossom
NECKLACE

The screen finding that attaches the wired flower to strands of simple stringing makes this necklace look seamless.

Bead store

 5 g light pink size 11° seed beads and 5 g medium pink size 11° seed beads

 5 g dark pink size 11° seed beads

 2 g lime green size 11° seed beads

 15 g size 10° green hex-cut beads

 Flower-shaped accent bead

 6 leaf-shaped accent beads

Screen finding with three attaching points

Beading wire (28 gauge) and beading needle

15in
38cm

1 Cut 24" (61 cm) of wire and bend over about 6" (15 cm) at one end. String 25 light pink seed beads, dropping them down to the bend in the wire. Bend the wire around to meet the first bend. Twist the wires together to form the first petal.

2 Repeat three more times, so there are four petals in the first layer.

3 Work a second layer of four petals, each with 20 medium pink beads. Work a third layer of four petals, each with 15 dark pink beads. Make a final layer, each with 10 dark pink beads.

4 Pass the accent bead and 1 medium pink bead down to the last row of petals. Skipping the seed bead, pass back through the accent bead and the layers of petals. Twist around the stem wire to secure. Thread the stem wire down through the screen finding and bend over to secure.

5 Cut six 4" (10 cm) lengths of wire. Pass 1 leaf bead and 1 green seed bead down to the center of one length. Skipping the seed bead, pass the end of the wire back through the leaf bead. Twist the wire ends together. Repeat.

6 Remove the screen disk of the finding. Attach the first leaf by splitting the pair of wires and fitting them into adjacent holes on the edge. Turn the clasp over, twist the wires, and bend them flat onto the back. Trim ends.

7 Apply the screen disk to the base of the clasp and clamp in place using flat-nose pliers.

8 Add a string of green size 10° hex beads to each of the three clasp eyes on both sides of the clasp.

petals
NECKLACE

What a difference colored wire makes to a simply strung necklace! Not many pink beads were used, but the pink core gives the appearance of a fresh summer garden.

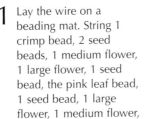

Bead store

 12 pink size 11° seed beads

 6 medium bell-shaped green flowers

 4 large bell-shaped pale green flowers

 Pink leaf bead

 6 silver crimp beads

2 silver knot cups

Clasp

40" (1 m) plastic-coated beading wire

2 Center the set of beads and crimp both crimp beads to secure.

1 Lay the wire on a beading mat. String 1 crimp bead, 2 seed beads, 1 medium flower, 1 large flower, 1 seed bead, the pink leaf bead, 1 seed bead, 1 large flower, 1 medium flower, 2 seed beads, and 1 crimp bead.
➤ **Simple stringing, see page 132**

3 On one side, string 1 crimp bead, 1 seed bead, 1 medium flower, 1 large flower, 1 medium flower, 2 seed beads, and 1 crimp bead.

4 Leaving a gap of about 1" (2.5 cm) crimp the crimp beads on either side of this set of beads in place. Complete the other side of the necklace to match.

5 Apply the knot cups and the clasp to the ends of the necklace.

16in
41cm

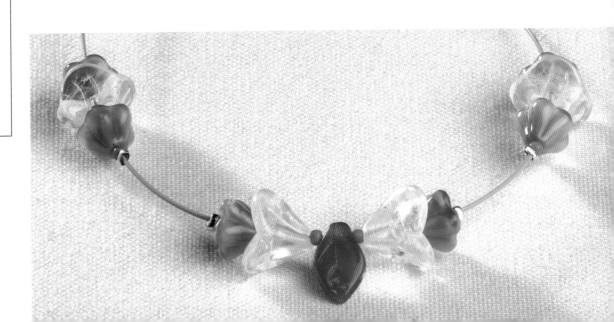

doily buttons

NECKLACE AND BRACELET

This design focuses on lovely antique buttons, framed in flat, circular peyote stitch, and hung on a simple beaded rope.

Bead store

Necklace

30 g purple size 11° seed beads

20 g blue size 11° seed beads

5 g blue size 15° seed beads

6 Buttons

Clasp

Beading needle and thread

Bracelet

20 g purple size 11° seed beads

20 g blue size 11° seed beads

5 g blue size 15° seed beads

4 to 5 buttons

Beading needle and thread

NECKLACE

1 Thread up 40" (1 m) of thread. String 10 purple beads, and join in a circle. Double-knot. Pass the tail of the thread through the next 2 or 3 beads in the circle. Trim close to work.

2 Work in flat, circular peyote stitch using blue beads. To step up, pass needle through the first bead again. Continue in peyote stitch.
➤ **Peyote stitch, see page 114**

3 String 2 purple beads between each blue bead of previous row. Pass needle through first 2 beads again.

4 String a blue bead between each bead (including each pair) of previous row. Pass needle through first bead again.

5 String 2 purple beads between each blue bead. Pass needle through first bead again.

6 String a blue bead between each pair of purple beads. Pass the needle through the first bead again. Then work as Step 3.

7 String a blue bead between each bead. Pass the needle through the first bead again. Then work as Step 8 and then as Step 3.

8 String a blue bead between each bead. Pass needle through the first 2 beads again. String 2 blue beads between each bead.

9 Pass thread back into center of work and secure. Pass around the shank of a button and back into work. Repeat several times to secure.

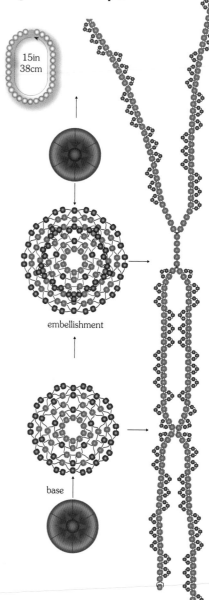

15in 38cm

embellishment

base

10 Double over 60" (1.5 m) of thread. Pass both ends through eye of needle. Pass through one end of clasp and through loop. Pull to secure. String enough beads to work one side of the rope.

11 Pass the needle through shank of first button. String 20 purple beads. Pass through shank of second button.

12 String 25 purple beads for first "tail." Skip the last bead. Pass back up through beads and last button added. String 19 purple beads. Pass through first button.

13 String beads for the second section. Pass around the clasp. Using 3 size 15° beads, work a picot on each alternate bead.
➤ **Picot edging, see page 136**

14 Pass down past the last button. Add a second tail using 17 purple beads. Pass back up, adding picots.

BRACELET

1 Work a length of netting.
➤ **Netting stitch, see page 122**

2 Work 4 or 5 doily buttons, then attach to netting.

3 The final doily button sits at the very edge of the bracelet, and a beaded loop is worked at the other end.

CHOKERS

textured brick stitch

CHOKER AND EARRINGS

This choker and earrings in beads of the same tones shows how effective texture and shape can be. Work it in ladder stitch with a row of brick stitch on either side. Use the beads listed in any combination. The matching earrings are simple drops. Remember to turn the work through the earring finding.

13in
33cm

Bead store

Choker

 Size 11° seed beads

Size 15° seed beads

Double-size cylinder beads

6mm bugle beads

Accent beads

Beading needle and thread

Earrings

Use the same materials as for the choker but vary the amounts of beads as required.

CHOKER

1 Thread the needle with about 60" (1.5 m) of thread. String 3 or 4 bugle beads and work in ladder stitch. Use any combination of stacks of beads that add up to about the same length. Work two or three repeats using the same type of bead. Continue to the length required.

2 Work brick stitch through the top and bottom loops of the core row. Bring the needle up through the first bead, and add 2 bugles. Secure the first two bugles by working the "locking stitch."
➤➤ **Brick stitch, see page 119**

3 Continue in brick stitch, adding beads or stacks of beads.

4 Work brick stitch on the other side of the core row, mirroring the pattern used for the first brick stitch row.

5 Leave the piece as it is or, for extra texture, pick out beads or groups of beads and add the same over the top for a raised effect. Accent beads may also be added at this point.

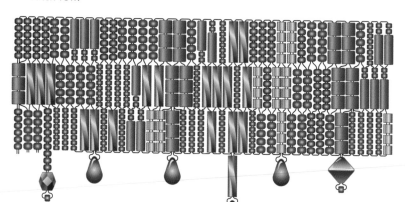

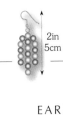

2in
5cm

EARRINGS

1 Thread the needle using about 40" (1 m) of thread. Attach to an earring finding with a double knot. String 5 seed beads, 3 double cylinder beads, 5 size 11° seed beads, 2 double cylinder beads, 5 size 11° seed beads, and an accent bead.

2 Add 4 size 11° seed beads. Pass the needle back through the first bead of the last set of size 11° beads added. Pass through the 2 larger beads.

3 Continue to add further "sets" of beads, taking the needle through odd beads on the first row as you work, to secure them.

4 Make three or four passes back and forth, until the earring has a nice shape and enough weight.

Victorian choker
NECKLACE

The style of this choker dates back to Victorian Britain. Choosing different colors, design one for day and one for evening.

Bead store

 15 g size 8° seed beads

 10 g size 11° seed beads

 20 small accent beads with horizontal holes

Clasp

Beading needle and thread

13in
34cm

1 Thread the needle using about 60" (1.5 m) of thread. Work the choker band in peyote stitch, 4 size 8° beads across on the initial row. Attach the clasp to both ends.
➤ **Peyote stitch, see page 114**
➤ **Attaching a clasp, see page 140**

2 Fold the choker band in half to find the center, and mark with a pin. Thread the needle using about 60" (1.5 m) of thread. Lay the band flat with the pin still in place. Count 2 beads from the center, and take the needle down through the band from the top vertically. Secure using a double knot.

3 To place the fringe beads, work the center "swag," then the medium, small, and smallest swags. Each sits slightly overlapping the next.

4 Repeat Steps 1 to 3 for the opposite side.

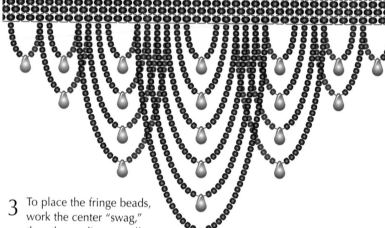

right-angle weave
— CHOKER —

Right-angle weave is a stunning stitch, especially when you work it in squares. For this design, fill the squares with 4mm cubes, and introduce the crystals for just a hint of sparkle.

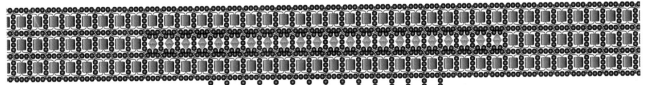

13in
34cm

Bead store

- Up to 30 g size 11° seed beads

- 20 g 4mm cubes

- 61 4mm crystals

- 2 fire-polished 6mm beads for bead and loop fastening

Beading needle and thread

1 Thread the needle with about 60" (1.5 m) of thread. Work in square right-angle weave, three squares across, using seed beads. Work enough rows to go round the neck as a choker.
➤ **Right-angle weave, see page 129**

2 Lay the finished "mesh" on a flat surface. Set aside enough crystals for the fringes. Count the number of cubes needed at either end of the middle row, as the crystals should be central.

3 Fill in the squares by adding cubes or crystals as appropriate.

4 Add the fringes between the two lower squares, beginning between the fourth and the fifth crystal in.
➤ **Adding a fringe, see page 137**

5 Add a bead and loop fastener.
➤ **Attaching a clasp, see page 140**

cool cubes

CHOKER AND BRACELET

This choker has a classic, uncluttered look with simple lines. For an amazing contemporary look, add another row of cubes to each side, and embellish with bugles, seed beads, and crystals. The base for the matching bracelet is a wider version of the choker.

Bead store

Choker

30 g 4mm cubes (main color)

10 g 4mm cubes (accent color)

Clasp

Beading needle and thread

14in
35cm

Bracelet

20 g 4mm cubes (main color)

10 g 4mm cubes (accent color)

10 g 6mm bugles in each of three complementary colors

15 g size 11° seed beads

12 4mm crystals

Beading needle and thread

NECKLACE

1 Thread needle with 60" (1.5 m) of thread. Using cubes in the main color, work a bead ladder long enough to fit the neck.
➤ **Ladder stitch, see page 118**

2 Pick up 2 cubes, working the "locking stitch."
➤ **Brick stitch, see page 119 and note on page 120.**

3 Work along the row in brick stitch to the last loop, and place a cube on it. At each end of the choker, the middle row is slightly longer, which helps the clasp sit neatly.

4 Beginning at either end, pass the needle down through the first cube, and bring it through with the thread facing the middle cube. Pick up an accent color cube, and pass the needle through the cube on the opposite outside edge.

5 Pass the needle down through the next cube. Pick up an accent color cube, and pass through the corresponding cube on the other outside edge. Continue to end.

6 Attach the clasp in the usual way.
➤ **Attaching a clasp, see page 140**

BRACELET

1 Work a basic bracelet as for the choker, adding an extra row of cubes to each side of the base. Add a top row of cubes in the accent color.

2 Embellish the work by making tiny "stalks" from 1 or 2 bugle beads. Attach them by passing the needle in and out of the top cubes. Add a seed bead to the end of each "stalk." When each cube is full (four or five "stalks"), move to the next cube.

3 Add a final row of crystals, working through the cubes as you add them.

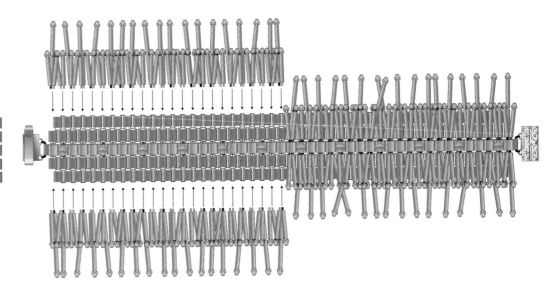

7in
18cm

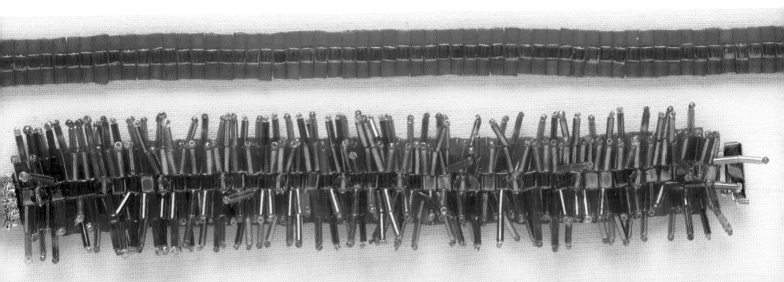

perfect pearls

CHOKER AND BRACELET

Simple, unfussy lines are often the best, and this classic pearl choker in right-angle weave is a must. Remember to allow for the clasp when gauging the length. Fringes embellish the bracelet for a different, but complementary effect.

CHOKER

1 Using about 40" (1 m) of thread and leaving an 8" (20 cm) tail, work a band of pearls in single right-angle weave to the required length.
➤➤ **Right-angle weave, see page 129**

2 Pass the tail end back up and through one side of the clasp. Pass back through the same side of the pearl you emerged from initially, and to the other side.

3 Pass through the other side of the clasp, then back up through the pearl again. Repeat two or three times, alternately going down and coming up through the clasp. This ensures that the clasp sits flat to the neck.

14in
35cm

Bead store

Choker

15 g cream 4mm pearls

Two-bar clasp

Beading needle and thread

Bracelet

15 g cream 4mm faux pearls

10 g cream size-11° seed beads

Two-bar clasp

Beading needle and thread

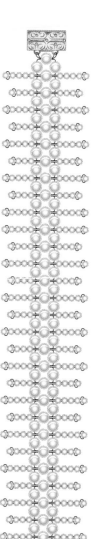

BRACELET

1 Using about 40" (1 m) of thread and the faux pearls, make a single right-angle weave band in the appropriate length.

2 Attach the clasp as for the choker.

3 To embellish the bracelet, bring the working thread out from the first bead in the center row. String 5 seed beads. Skip the last bead and pass back through the seed beads and the central pearl. Make another strand of fringe on the other side of the pearl.

4 Take the needle around the next "set" of pearls to the next central bead. String 4 seed beads to make a strand of fringe. Repeat on the other side of the pearl.

5 Continue adding this fringe all along the row, alternating 4 or 5 seed beads.

6 Add the second half of the clasp.
➤ **Attaching a clasp, see page 140**

7in
18cm

simple elegance

CHOKER AND BROOCH

13in
34cm

This choker combines simplicity, elegance, and beauty. For a perfect fringe, hold up the necklace as you add each strand. If your work is too loose, the beading thread will show and the beads will not sit snugly against the choker. If it is too tight, the fringe will buckle, pull, and spoil the effect. The brooch complements the choker perfectly.

Bead store

Choker

10 g size 11° seed beads

10 g 6mm bugle beads

Clasp

Beading needle and thread

Brooch

10 g size 11° seed beads

5 g 6mm bugle beads

40 4mm fire-polished crystals

1½ in (3 cm) brooch back

Beading needle and thread

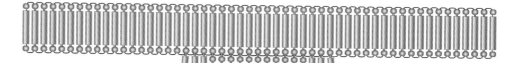

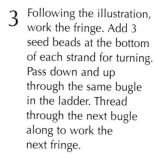

CHOKER

1 Thread the needle using about 60" (1.5 m) of thread. Work a bead ladder to fit neck using bugle beads. Discard any beads that are not cleanly cut or have a rough edge, as they may cut the thread.
➤ **Ladder stitch, see page 118**

2 Fold the ladder in half to find the center. The fringe has 17 strands, so count 9 bugles from the center and pass through the relevant bead.

3 Following the illustration, work the fringe. Add 3 seed beads at the bottom of each strand for turning. Pass down and up through the same bugle in the ladder. Thread through the next bugle along to work the next fringe.
➤ **Adding a fringe, see page 137**

4 Using size 11° seed beads, work a row of brick stitch along each edge of the choker, skipping the fringe section. Add a clasp.
➤ **Brick stitch, see page 119**
➤ **Adding a clasp, see page 140**

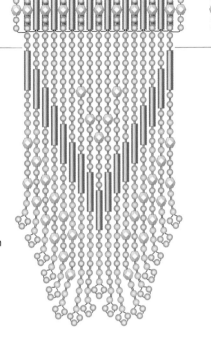

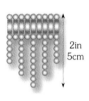

BROOCH

1 Thread the needle using about 60" (1.5 m) of thread. Work a bead ladder, 17 bugles long.

2 Pass up through the first bugle. String 2 seed beads, 1 crystal, and 2 seed beads. Pass through the second bugle.

3 Turn, and pass back down through the beads just added. Pass back up through the first bugle again to fix the beads between the 2 bugles with a cross-stitch. Pass down through the second bugle again, and then up through the third bugle. Continue until all the bugles are embellished.

2in
5cm

4 Following the diagram, add the fringes in the same way as the choker.

5 Work a row of brick stitch along the top of the bugle ladder with size 11° beads.

6 Stitch through both the top row of seed beads and the bottom edge of the bugle beads to attach the brooch back.

14in
35cm

Bead store

Choker

 20 g size 10° triangles

 10 g size 11° seed beads in each of two colors

 Star-shaped accent beads

Beading needle and thread

Ring

 5 g blue-green size 11° seed beads

8 matte aqua star accent beads

Beading needle and thread

swinging stars
CHOKER AND RING

The lovely sparkle that radiates from this choker comes from triangles that reflect the light beautifully. Stars swing freely on randomly placed "swags" at the front. You can embellish the ring at any point.

CHOKER

1 Thread the needle using about 60" (1.5 m) of thread. Work a rectangular strip of peyote stitch, 10 beads wide, to fit the neck.
▶ **Peyote stitch, see page 114**

2 Attach the clasp before you finish off the threads at each end of the work. This will help to secure the choker when you are deciding how many "swags" to add.
▶ **Attaching a clasp, see page 140**

3 Find the rough center of the choker, and begin to add swags to the front. Place a few to begin with, then add more, checking to see if there are any gaps. Stop when you have reached the size you are happy with.

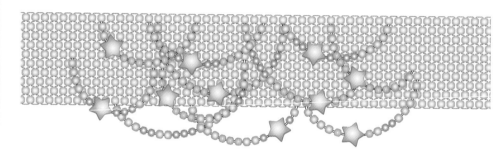

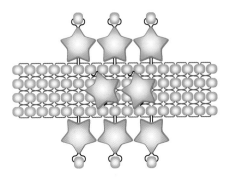

RING

4 Finish off.
➤ **Starting and finishing threads, see page 138**

1 Using about 40" (1 m) of thread and the seed beads, work a length of square stitch, 4 beads across. Continue until work fits around the finger. Square-stitch the ends together.
➤ **Square stitch, see page 125**

2 Bring the needle out through one of the beads on the outside edge. String 1 star and 1 seed bead. Pass back through the star and into the body of the beadwork.

3 Weave in and out of beads to the point where another star is to be placed. Add 2 more stars in the same way. Repeat on the opposite side of the ring.

4 Attach 2 more stars to the top of the ring. Finish off.

2½in
6cm

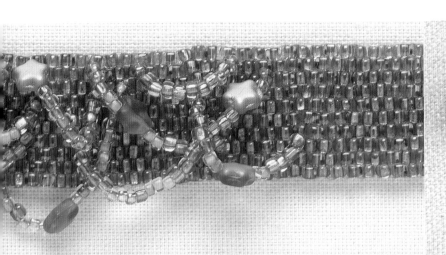

dragonfly
CHOKER

16in
41cm

Bead store

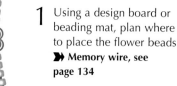

20 g size 8° blue seed beads

4 large flower beads with horizontal holes

6 small flower beads with horizontal holes

Dragonfly bead

Memory wire

Flat-nose pliers

Take time to plan this magical memory-wire necklace, as the size and graduation of beads is key to its design.

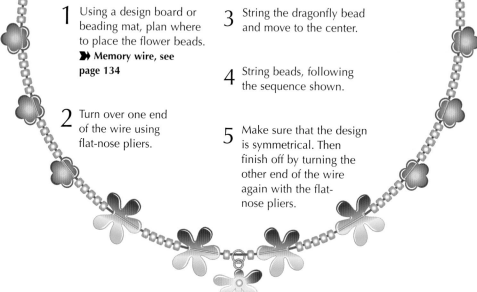

1 Using a design board or beading mat, plan where to place the flower beads.
➤ **Memory wire, see page 134**

2 Turn over one end of the wire using flat-nose pliers.

3 String the dragonfly bead and move to the center.

4 String beads, following the sequence shown.

5 Make sure that the design is symmetrical. Then finish off by turning the other end of the wire again with the flat-nose pliers.

mauve rocks

CHOKER

This memory-wire choker is made from sleek glass beads. To help you try out lots of ideas, use a bead board, a beading mat, or even just a piece of soft fabric.

17in
43cm

Bead store

5 g size 6° purple seed beads

Mauve glass beads in assorted shapes and sizes

Choker-length memory wire

Flat-nose pliers

1 Turn one end of the wire over with flat-nose pliers.
➤ **Memory wire, see page 134**

2 Add beads to create one side of the design, checking that they go well together.

3 Graduate the beads down from the center, adding a seed bead between each of the glass beads in the front section to inject some brighter color.

4 Repeat for the second side of the choker, mirroring the design of the first side. Turn the second end over with pliers to complete.

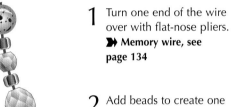

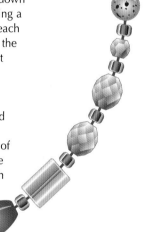

crystal greens
CHOKER AND BROOCH

Matte seed beads complement the crystals, which can be fastened at the back or front. The fringes can be any length, but remember they need to be able to fit through the loop at the end of the choker! The brooch is the perfect complement to the crystal greens choker.

CHOKER

1 Using about 40" (1 m) of thread, string a crystal and 14 seed beads. Pass the needle back through the crystal to form a fastening loop. Pass the needle back through all the beads. Using the tail end and the working thread, work a double knot between the beads. Continue around until your thread is coming out of the crystal.

2 *String 3 beads, 1 crystal, 3 beads, 1 crystal, 3 beads, 1 crystal, and 3 beads. Pass back through the crystal strung in Step 1. Pass through 3 beads, 1 crystal, 3 beads, and 1 crystal.

3 String 3 beads, 1 crystal, and 3 beads. Pass through the last crystal in the opposite direction, then through 3 beads and 1 crystal.

4 String 3 beads, 1 crystal, and 3 seed beads. Pass back through the last crystal, then through 3 beads and 1 crystal. Repeat from * until the required length is reached.

5 String 5 beads. Pass back through the crystal to form a loop of beads around its outside end. Pass back through the first 3 beads in the loop. String 1 bead, 1 crystal, 1 bead, 1 crystal, and 1 bead. Fasten the loop at the other end over a crystal, using whichever crystal gives you the most comfortable fit.

6 For the longest strand of fringing, string 12 beads, 1 crystal, and 6 beads. Pass back through the first of the 6 beads added. Continue to thread back up the fringe.
➤ Adding a fringe, see page 137

7 String two more strands of fringes, each using 13 beads. Pass the needle back up through the fourth bead from the bottom and back up the beading.

16in
41cm

Bead store

Choker

 10 g matte green size 11° seed beads

50 to 60 fire-polished 6mm crystals

Beading needle and thread

Brooch

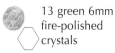 5 g matte green size 11° seed beads

13 green 6mm fire-polished crystals

Beading needle and thread

1" (2.5 cm) pin back

BROOCH

1 Using 40″ (1 m) of thread and leaving a 6″ (15 cm) tail, string 3 seed beads, 1 crystal, and 3 beads, and a crystal. Double-knot the tail end and working thread to form a circle. Pass through the top set of beads and a crystal.

2in
5cm

2 String * 3 beads, 1 crystal, and 3 beads. Pass the needle down through the previous crystal. Pass through the 3 beads and the crystal. Repeat from * until 6 crystals in total are strung.

3 Working from right to left, pass the needle down through the next to last crystal on the first row. String 1 bead, 1 crystal, 3 beads, 1 crystal, and 1 bead. Pass the needle back up through to the third crystal on the initial row.

4 Pass the needle through the next 3 beads on the top row, then down through the fourth crystal on the initial row. String 1 bead, 1 crystal, 3 beads, 1 crystal, and 1 bead.

5 Pass back up through to the fifth crystal on the initial row, then the 3 beads to the right of the crystal. Pass down through the crystal, 1 bead, and 1 crystal. String 1 bead, 1 crystal, 3 beads, 1 crystal, and 1 bead.

6 Pass up through the second crystal on the right on the second row, and the 3 beads on the left of the crystal. Pass down through the third crystal, 1 bead, and the left crystal on the third row. Pass through the first and second beads on the bottom 3-bead loop.

7 Add the three fringes exactly as you did for the choker. Sew the pin back in position to finish.

Chinese choker
NECKLACE

Here is a dramatic mix of glass, wooden, and ceramic beads. The terra-cotta color of the seed beads brings out the tones in the feature beads.

Bead store

 10 g terra-cotta colored size 6° seed beads

 2 g terra-cotta colored size 11° seed beads

 3 large printed wooden beads

4 medium terra-cotta colored ceramic beads

Beading needle and thread

Magnetic clasp

14in
35cm

1 Double over 40" (1 m) of thread and pass both ends through the eye of the needle. Pass through one end of the clasp. As the loop forms, pass through and pull up to secure the thread to the clasp.
➤ **Attaching a clasp, see page 140**

2 String 5 size 11° seed beads, then string size 6° seed beads so the length reaches almost to the center.

3 String 1 ceramic bead, 1 wooden bead, 1 ceramic bead, 1 wooden bead, 1 ceramic bead, 1 wooden bead, and 1 ceramic bead.

4 Continue to string size 6° beads until each side of the choker is the same length, remembering to add 5 size 11° beads at the end.

5 Pass through the other end of the clasp, then pass back down through several beads. Double-knot between 2 beads, then pass through 2 more beads. Trim ends.

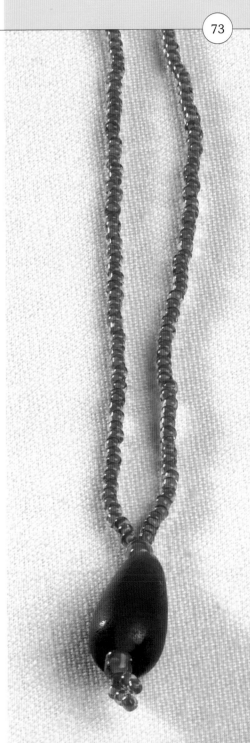

single drop
─ CHOKER ─

This great little choker may be made in any color to suit any outfit, and can be created in record time. Use a double thread for added strength and security.

Bead store

  10 g terra-cotta size 11° seed beads

2 terra-cotta size 6° seed beads

1 medium/large terra-cotta drop bead with a vertical hole

Magnetic clasp

Beading needle and thread

1 Double over 40" (1 m) of thread and pass both ends through the needle.

2 Pass through the eye on one side of the clasp. As the loop starts to form, pass the needle through the loop and pull up to secure the thread to the clasp.

3 String size 11° seed beads to reach the center where the single drop bead will sit.

4 String 1 size 6° seed bead, 1 drop bead, 1 size 6° bead, and 6 size 11° seed beads. Pass through the first of the last 6 seed beads added to form a loop at the base of the drop bead. Pass up through the size 6° bead, the drop bead, and the second size 6° bead.
➤➤ **Beaded loops, see page 135**

5 Pull up the thread so no excess shows between the first length of choker and the drop section. String size 11° beads to complete the second half of the choker.

6 Pass the needle up through the eye on the other end of the clasp, then back down through several beads. Double-knot between two beads. Pass through several more beads and trim the ends.

14in
35cm

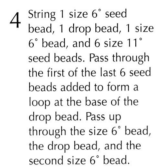

sun god
CHOKER

The tantalizing accent beads inspired this choker. Matte and shiny beads are a winning combination, and the band of hex beads adds sparkle.

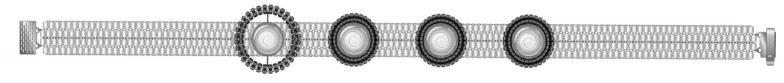

14in
35cm

Bead store

  10 g size 11° seed beads in earth tones

 20 g size 10° lime-green hex beads

5 round accent beads

2-bar clasp

Beading needle and thread

1 Using about 40" (1 m) of thread, pass the needle through one of the accent beads leaving a 6" (15 cm) tail. String 16 seed beads (or enough to go halfway around your accent bead). Pass through the opposite end of the accent bead.

2 String the same amount of beads. Pass through the opposite end of the accent bead to surround the center bead with a circle of beads.

3 Pass the needle through all the seed beads. Secure with a double knot.

4 Work flat circular peyote stitch through the seed beads surrounding the accent bead.
➤➤ **Peyote stitch, see page 114**

5 Work a second row of peyote stitch, keeping the beadwork flat. Finish off. Work four more motifs in exactly the same way.

6 Work the band for the motifs in ladder stitch using two hex beads instead of the usual bugle bead. When it is the length required, add a row of brick stitch to the top and the bottom.
➤➤ **Ladder stitch, see page 118**
➤➤ **Brick stitch, see page 119**

7 Sew the five motifs in place, then attach the clasp.
➤➤ **Attaching a clasp, see page 140**

blue slates
CHOKER

These slate sections from a Cornish beach are wonderfully smooth. For the best effect, they should graduate slightly in size.

14in
35cm

Bead store

 10 g ocean-blue size 6° seed beads

 5 g ocean-blue size 11° seed beads

7 sections of drilled slate (or beach glass)

Toggle clasp

Beading needle and thread

1 Attach one side of the clasp using 60″ (1.5 m) of thread.
➤ **Attaching a clasp, see page 140**

2 Using both strands of thread, string 4 size 11° beads, then size 6° beads to 1½″ (4 cm) from the center of the choker.

3 String a small slate section from back to front. String 6 size 11° beads. Pass back through the first bead to make a loop, then to the back of the slate. String 3 size 6° beads and pull up.

4 String a second slate section, using 10 size 11° beads for the loop. String 3 size 6° beads. String a third slate section, using 14 size 11° beads. String 3 size 6° beads. String the central slate section, using 16 beads. String 3 size 6° beads.

5 Work the second half of the necklace to mirror the first. Add the second half of the clasp. Turn.

6 Pass through the 4 size 11° beads. Double-knot the thread and work with one strand. Pass through the beads to the front of the first slate section. String 10 size 11° beads.

7 Pass through the bead loop on the second slate section. Catch the first loop again, then pass through the first slate section and the next 3 beads. Work loops of 12, 14, and 16 size 11° beads. Complete, decreasing the size of the loops as the slates get smaller, until each loop on the first row is joined by a second-stage loop. Pass through the size 6° beads and finish.

daisy pinks
CHOKER

The classy daisy is the focal point for this simply strung, yet elegant, choker. If you want to twist the strands, make it a little longer.

14in
35cm

Bead store

15 g assorted pink size 11° seed beads

Focal flower bead or button with a shank

Clasp

Beading needle and thread

1 Double over 40" (1 m) of thread and pass both ends through the needle. Pass through one end of the clasp. As the loop forms, pass through and pull up to secure the thread to the clasp.
➤ **Attaching a clasp, see page 140**

2 String seed beads to reach the center front of the choker.

3 Pass the thread through the connector or shank at the back of the daisy.

4 String seed beads until the second half of the choker is the same length as the first.

5 Pass the needle through the second half of the clasp. Pass it back down through several beads. Double-knot between 2 beads, then pass through 2 more. Trim ends.

6 String two more rows of beads as before. Finish off.
➤ **Starting and finishing threads, see page 138**

pearl sweetheart
CHOKER

This timeless pearl choker is simple yet stunningly beautiful, with blush pink faux pearls that complement any skin tone.

Bead store

 10 to 15 blush pink 8mm faux pearls

 90 to 120 blush pink 6mm faux pearls

Clasp

Beading needle and thread

14in 35cm

1 Double over 40" (1 m) of thread. Pass both ends through the needle.

2 Pass through the eye on one half of the clasp. As the loop forms, pass the needle through and pull on the thread to secure it to the clasp.

3 Place a needle on each end of the thread, and pass both needles through an 8mm pearl.

4 * String five 6mm pearls on each thread, then pass both needles through an 8mm pearl. Repeat from * until the choker is the required length, passing both needles through an 8mm pearl to finish.

5 Check the length. If it is too long, remove 1 or 2 pearls from the last section, or reduce the number of pearls used for each section.

6 Pass one of the needles through the eye on the second half of the clasp, then back into the bead stringing. Double-knot the thread and pass through 2 or 3 more beads. Trim ends.

7 Repeat with the second thread. Finish off.
➤ **Starting and finishing threads, see page 138**

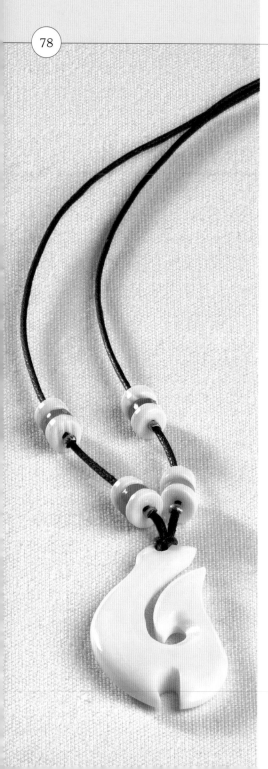

whale watch

CHOKER

Make the boldest statement with the simple language of beads: this beautiful whale-shaped pendant says it all.

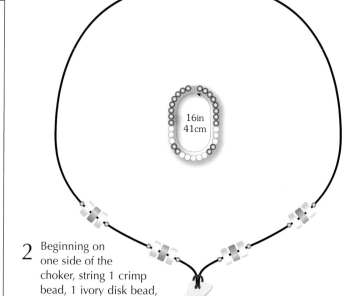

Bead store

 4 beige disk beads

 8 ivory disk beads

  8 gold crimp beads

1 pendant

2 jump rings

2 flat leather crimp ends

1 lobster clasp

Waxed cotton bead cord

Flat-nose pliers

1 Pass both ends of the cord through the front of the pendant. As a loop forms, pass the two ends through and pull up to secure.

2 Beginning on one side of the choker, string 1 crimp bead, 1 ivory disk bead, 1 beige disk, 1 ivory disk, and 1 crimp bead. Crimp the crimp beads in place using pliers.
➤ **Crimping, see page 134**

3 String a second "set" of beads further up the choker. Repeat on the opposite side.

4 Cut the cord to the length required. Pass one end into a flat leather crimp and clamp in place. Repeat for the other side.

5 Open a jump ring slightly. Pass the open ring through the eye on the leather crimp bead, adding the lobster clasp at the same time. Close the jump ring.

6 Attach a jump ring to the other side of the choker to finish.

ancient shell

—— CHOKER ——

The focal shell on this choker was in the sea for so long it has been worn almost flat and wonderfully smooth.

Bead store

 15 g silver-gray size 8° seed beads

 10 g silver-gray size 11° seed beads

 10 g charcoal-gray size 11° seed beads

Focal shell
   with drilled hole

Clasp

Beading needle and
   thread

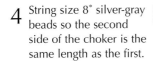

16in
41cm

3 String 1 silver-gray size 8° bead and 12 silver-gray size 11° beads. Work a line of branch fringing. Pass back through the size 8° bead and to the back of the shell.

4 String size 8° silver-gray beads so the second side of the choker is the same length as the first.

1 Double over 60″ (1.5 m) of thread and attach the clasp in the usual way. String 5 silver-gray size 11° beads, then string size 8° silver-gray beads to reach the center point.

2 Pass through the drilled hole in the focal shell, from the back to the front.
➤ **Drilling, see page 134**

5 Pass the needle through the second half of the clasp to the first size 8° bead. Double-knot between the two beads.

6 Leave one thread aside and work with the other. Pass through to within 30 size 8° beads of the center shell.

7 Work back and forth adding to the branch fringing until you are happy with the effect.

dichroic triangle

CHOKER AND BROOCH

Dichroic beads come in all shapes and sizes, and it can be quite a challenge to incorporate them in a piece of jewelry. To complement this triangle, less was definitely more. When you make this brooch, use your eye to judge how long to make the sections of fringe.

CHOKER

1 Using about 40" (1 m) of thread, work a length of bugle ladder to make a comfortable choker.
➤ **Ladder stitch, see page 118**

Bead store

Choker	**Brooch**
10 g bright purple size 11° seed beads	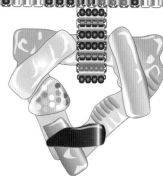
10 g pink size 11° seed beads	
10 g bright green size 15° seed beads	
20 g clear 6mm bugle beads	

Choker

 10 g bright purple size 11° seed beads

 10 g pink size 11° seed beads

 10 g bright green size 15° seed beads

 20 g clear 6mm bugle beads

Dichroic triangle bead

Two-bar clasp

Beading needle and thread

Brooch

 5 g bright purple size 11° seed beads

 5 g bright pink size 11° seed beads

 5 g bright green size 15° seed beads

 5 g clear 6mm bugle beads

1" (2.5 cm) pin back

Beading needle and thread

14in 35cm

---

2 Working flat, bring the needle out at the top of the outside bugle. Using any of the bright colors, string 4 size 11° beads. Pass through the opposite end of the next bugle along to create a diagonal stitch. String 4 size 11° beads. Pass through the opposite end of the next bugle to create a diagonal stitch.

3 Pass down through the 4 bright beads. Bring the needle back up through the first bugle to form a "cross-stitch." Pass back through the second bugle.

4 Add sets of bright beads, in any order, over the bugles. Secure the dichroic bead to the "tab" section by passing through the first and last bugle added.

5 Attach the dichroic triangle to the central bugle on the choker. Secure the thread by passing from the top bugle on the tab, backward and forward through the bugles on either side of the central bead, two or three times.

6 Attach the clasp.
➤ **Attaching a clasp, see page 140**

BROOCH

1 Using about 40" (1 m) of thread and 21 bugle beads, make a bugle ladder. Using bright purple beads, work a row of brick stitch on top.

2 Using the bright beads, embellish the bugle beads as for the choker. Pass down through the next bugle on either side of the central bugle.

3 String 4 pink seed beads for the first strand of fringing. Skip the last bead added and pass the needle back through the third bead added. String 2 more pink beads. Skip the central bugle, and pass through the next bugle along on the opposite side.
▶ Adding a fringe, see page 137

4 Continue to add fringing, threading back and forth and from side to side, using the colors in any combination.

5 Attach the pin back by sewing it to the back of the beadwork.

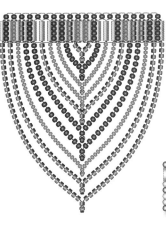

2in
5cm

petal rope leaf
LARIAT AND EARRINGS

Ropes are a popular choice since they are so easy to wear. This design has a summery feel, and the pale pink leaves add delicate detail to the ends. These pretty summer earrings complement the pink spiral rope lariat.

Bead store

Lariat

 10 g dark pink size 11° seed beads

 30 g light pink size 11° seed beads (bead mix)

10 light pink acrylic leaves

Beading needle and thread

Earrings

 5 g mixed pink size 11° seed beads

 6 light pink acrylic leaves

 6 bright pink acrylic leaves

Earring wires

Beading needle and thread

LARIAT

1 Thread the needle using about 40" (1 m) of thread. String 4 dark seed beads and 3 light beads. Tie into a circle using a double knot, leaving an 8" (20 cm) tail. Pass back through the 4 dark beads.

2 String 1 dark, 3 light beads * let the beads drop down to the initial circle. Pass the needle through the last 3 dark beads and the dark bead just added. Pull up the thread. Position the beads just added by the 3 outside beads added previously. String 1 dark bead and 3 light beads. Repeat from * until work measures at least 30" (76 cm).

3 Pass through the last 3 outside beads at the end of the rope. Add 20 beads and a leaf. Pass back up through the 20 beads and the 3 beads on the rope. Pass down through the next 3 outside beads. String 15 beads and a leaf. Return as before. Repeat, stringing 10 beads, 5 beads, and finally just a leaf, to give five strands of fringing in total. Complete the other end of the rope to match.

➤➤ **Adding a fringe, see page 137**

16in
41cm

3

2

1

Build up of the spiral rope

EARRINGS

1 Double-knot 12" (30 cm) of thread to the loop on the earring wire, leaving a 4" (10 cm) tail end.

2 String 20 beads, 1 light pink leaf, 3 beads, 1 bright pink leaf, 3 beads, and 1 light pink leaf, so the leaves face the line of 20 beads already strung.

3 String 3 beads, 1 bright pink leaf, 3 beads, 1 light pink leaf, 3 beads, and 1 bright pink leaf, so the leaves face in the opposite way (all 6 leaves face outward).

4 String 19 beads. Pass back through the first bead of the initial 20 beads strung. Pass back through the loop on the earring wire, then back down through several beads. Double-knot between 2 beads to secure. Pass through 2 more beads. Trim ends.

5 Thread needle on the tail end. Finish off.
➤➤ **Starting and finishing threads, see page 138**

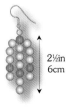

2½in
6cm

beaded red
NECKLACE

A simple but effective necklace to wear anytime. All six strands of embroidery floss are used, and you will need a special wire twisted needle with a collapsible eye that allows you to thread beads on to fairly thick thread.

Bead store

20 g bead soup mixture (size 8° and 6° seed beads, and decorative beads up to 8mm)

10 g matching or toning size 11° seed beads

One larger accent bead

Wire threading needle

Long beading needle

1 skein six-strand embroidery floss

1   Measure the length of embroidery floss required to make a comfortable lariat. Add 8″ (20 cm) to allow for finishing and/or length adjustment.

2   Thread the wire needle with all six strands of cotton.

3   Add the bead mixture randomly, leaving an 8″ (20 cm) tail. Continue to the required length.

4   Pass the thread through the larger accent bead. Remove the needle and use it to thread the tail end. Pass it through the larger accent bead.

5   Unravel both lengths of embroidery thread so there are twelve separate strands. Thread the beading needle with the first strand and add size 11° seed beads. If you have any beads left, include a few on each strand.

6   When the first strand is long enough, skip the last bead added, bring the needle back up, and work a double knot between the next 2 beads.

7   Work each separate strand of thread until all twelve are beaded to form a tassel.

21in
53cm

black fringed
— LARIAT —

This lariat uses cylinder beads, which sit beautifully together. It drapes really well around the neck and when tied together.

Bead store

  30 g size 11° cylinder beads

16 accent beads with horizontal holes

Beading needle and thread

36in
91cm

1 Thread the needle with about 60″ (1.5 m) of thread. Work even-count peyote stitch using 8 beads threaded on to the initial row of beads using the cylinder beads.
➤ **Peyote stitch, see page 114**

2 When the lariat is long enough to drape around the neck, and tie over itself, add the tassel.

3 Pick up a cylinder bead, and work square stitch through both beads. Moving down, keep adding beads to work the first strand of fringe (18 beads in total).

4 Pass back up the first strand of fringe. Pass through to the second bead on the end of the lariat. Add 14 beads for the next strand of fringe, then 12 for the next.

5 Add 7 beads for each of the next two strands of fringe. Work the last three strands in reverse, using 12, then 14, and finally 18 beads (eight strands in total).

6 Work the fringes for the opposite side in the same way.

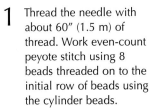

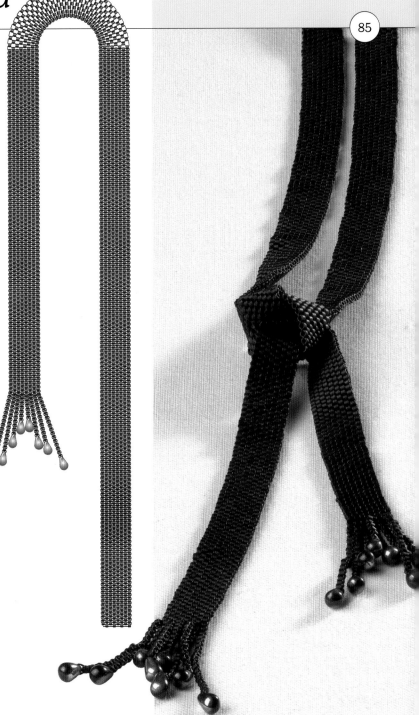

hearts cascade

LARIAT AND EARRINGS

These bright, passionate heart-shaped sequins seem to "float" in midair. You could also work the piece using glass accent beads. The stunning earrings can be made to any length you prefer.

LARIAT

1 Using 60" (1.5 m) of thread, pass a size 6° bead down to within 8" (20 cm) of the tail end. Pass the needle back through to create a stop bead.

2 String as many size 6° beads as required to make a comfortable lariat length. The lariat must be at least 30" (76 cm) long so the tassel ends show when it is worn. Turn.

3 String 5 size 11° beads, 1 pink heart, and 5 size 11° beads. Pass the needle back through the last size 6° bead added again.
➤ **Beaded loops, see page 135**

4 String 5 size 11° beads, a heart, and 5 more size 11° beads. Pass the needle through the next size 6° bead.

5 Continue adding the bead loops with sequins as desired, working a set between each size 6° bead. The example shows 4" (20 cm) of these bead loops.

6 Pass back through the beads to where you wish to resume adding bead loops. Complete to match the other end.

7 Before you reach the final bead on the second end, undo the stop bead loop. To finish off, knot between 2 beads, pass the needle through 2 or 3 more beads. Trim end.

Bead store

Lariat

 15 g dark purple size 6° seed beads

10 g dark purple size 11° seed beads

10 g bright pink heart-shaped sequins

Long beading needle and thread

Earrings

5 g dark purple size 11° seed beads

10 bright pink heart-shaped sequins

Earring wires

Beading needle and thread

15in 38cm

EARRINGS

1 Double-knot 40″ (1 m) of thread to a finding, leaving a 6″ (15 cm) tail.

2 String 1 heart, 9 beads, 1 heart, and 9 beads.

3 Pass through the top heart, back down through the first 9 beads and through the second heart.

4 String 9 beads, 1 heart, and 9 more beads. Pass back through the second heart in the ladder, then through the first 9 beads added in this set.

5 Add sets of beads as before until the earring is the length required. Place on the loop of the earwire. Finish off.
➤➤ **Starting and finishing a thread, see page 138**

6 Make another earring to match.

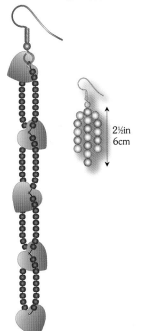

2½in
6cm

precious pearls
NECKLACE AND BRACELET

Pearls are always a favorite, whether you are casual or "dressed up."
Anything goes! The matching bracelet has six strings, each worked
separately. You can make it a little longer and twist it for a textured effect.

NECKLACE

1 Using 60" (1.5 m) of thread, and leaving a tail of 12" (30 cm), thread on * 5 cream seed beads, 10 faux pearls, repeat from * until the stringing reaches the required length for one half of the necklace.
➤ **Simple stringing, see page 132**

2 String 10 seed beads, passing the needle back up through the last 10 faux pearls.

3 String the second half of the necklace as before, adding 5 seed beads and 10 faux pearls until it matches the first half in length.

4 Attach a clasp to both ends.
➤ **Attaching a clasp, see page 140**

5 The necklace is now ready to be embellished. Add the various mother-of-pearl hearts by securing them to the groups of 5 seed beads. Bring the needle out of one of the 5 cream beads, thread on 5 cream or aqua beads, a heart, and 5 more beads. Thread back into the size 11 beads on the original stringing. This forms a loop from which the hearts hang prettily.

6 Place the hearts around the necklace and finish.

Bead store

Necklace

 10 g cream size 11° seed beads

 5 g aqua size 11° seed beads

 20 g 4mm faux pearls

Feature heart disk

Selection of small and medium mother-of-pearl hearts

Long beading needle and thread

Bracelet

15 g cream size 11° seed beads

15 g 4mm faux pearls

15 g faux pearl 5mm discs

Toggle clasp

Beading needle and thread

16in
41cm

7½in
19cm

BRACELET

1 Double over 40" (1 m) of thread and pass both ends through the needle. Pass through the fastening point on one end of the clasp. As the loop forms, pass through and pull firmly to secure.

2 String 5 seed beads, then pearls until the bracelet is the required length. Allow a little extra here if you want to twist the bracelet before wearing. String 5 more seed beads.

3 Pass the needle through the other end of the toggle clasp. Pass it back through the 5 seed beads and 2 or 3 pearls. Double-knot between 2 beads. Pass through 2 more beads. Trim thread.

4 Starting with a new length of thread, string a second row of pearls. Fasten off.

5 String a row of pearl discs. String two rows of seed beads. Finish off each row separately.

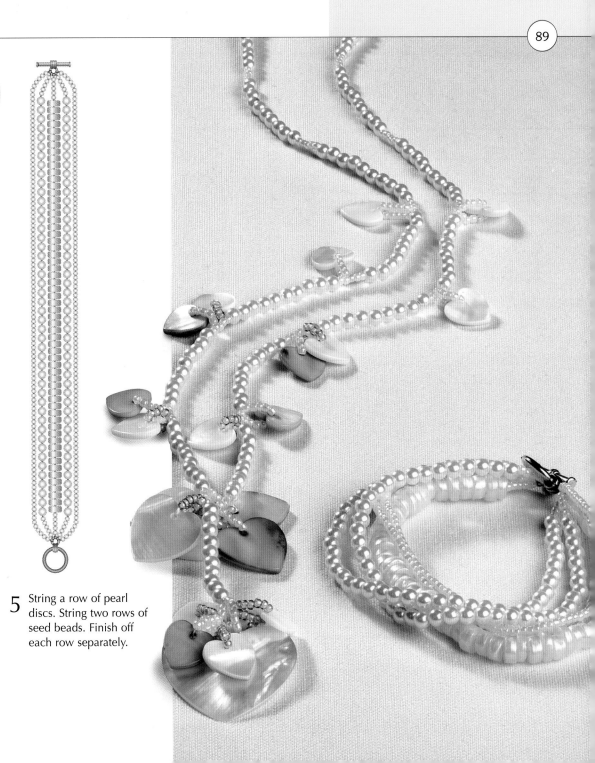

Chinese braid

NECKLACE

This simple yet stunning necklace uses beautiful Chinese-style beads, accented with deep red rats' tail.

Bead store

 9 large printed wooden beads

 14 medium printed wooden beads

60" (1.5 m) deep red rats' tail

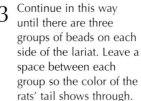

2 String 1 medium bead, 1 large bead, and 1 medium bead. Secure by making a double knot on the other side of this first group of beads.

3 Continue in this way until there are three groups of beads on each side of the lariat. Leave a space between each group so the color of the rats' tail shows through.

20in
51cm

4 Leaving a gap after the third group of beads, knot the rats' tail together with a single knot.

1 Lay the rats' tail flat. Leaving an 8–10" (20–25 cm) length for the back neck, double-knot to one side of the central space. One knot should sit directly over the other.
➡ **Knotting between beads, see page 139**

5 String 1 medium bead, 3 large beads, and 1 medium bead onto each of the two ends of rats' tail. Make another knot at the base of these beads. Trim ends.

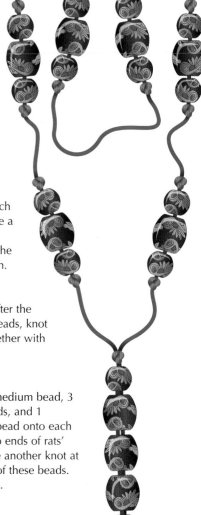

buttons

NECKLACE

Want a reason to dig out your button stash? Here you go! This design is easier to work if the first and each alternate button has four holes.

Bead store

Buttons in assorted shapes and sizes

Two 80" (2 m) lengths wax-coated cotton bead cord

21in
53cm

3 Lay the second length of cord beside the first. Pass the second length through the first button. If it has four holes, use either a "cross-stitch" or a "running-stitch" method.

4 String 1 or 2 buttons on the second length. These will sit between the first 2 buttons on the initial row. Pass the cord through the next button of the initial row.

5 Work in the same way along the length of cord. When the necklace is the length required, make a double knot. Trim ends.

1 Lay out the buttons and arrange them for effect.

2 String the buttons on a length of cord, leaving about 2" (5 cm) between each.

Japanese petal

NECKLACE AND EARRINGS

The dainty blue and green sequins combined with the seed beads create a delicate, feminine look to wear at the office or for an evening out. The simple looped earrings have clean lines that really complement the necklace. Make both pieces to create the perfect ensemble!

NECKLACE

1 Double-knot 60" (1.5 m) of thread to one end of the clasp leaving an 8" (20 cm) tail. String size 10° triangles to at least 12" (30 cm) long for the first side of the necklace. String a size 5° triangle, the focal bead, and the second size 5° triangle.

2 String 1 size 10° triangle and 1 sequin. Repeat until there are 15 sequins in total. Skipping the last triangle added, thread back through the first size 5° triangle and the focal bead, then the second size 5° triangle.

3 String size 10° triangles for the second side. Pass through the other half of the clasp, then back down into the triangles. Bring the needle out about 16 beads from the clasp.

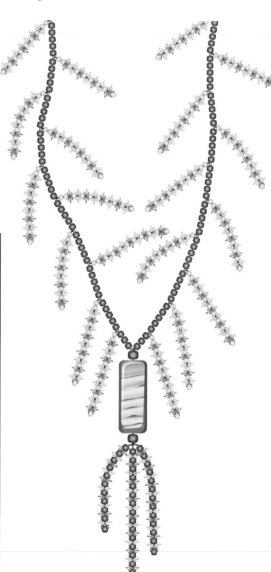

Bead store

Necklace

10 g lime-green size 11° seed beads

10 g green size 10° triangles

2 green size 5° triangles

10 g blue flower sequins

10 g green flower sequins

Focal bead

Toggle clasp

Beading needle and thread

26in 66cm

Earrings

5 g size 11° lime-green seed beads

24 blue flower sequins

24 green flower sequins

Earring wires

Beading needle and thread

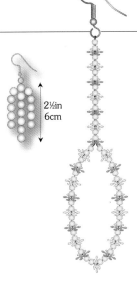

2½in
6cm

4 String 2 size 11° seed
beads, 1 blue sequin, 1
seed bead, 1 green
sequin, and 1 seed bead.
Skipping the last bead
added, pass back up
through the strand of
fringing and the next 5
triangles along. Work
three more strands using
the same sequence of
beads and sequins,
passing through 5
triangles each time.

5 Work four more strands
of 4 sequins with beads
between. Continue to
work sets of four strands,
adding 6, 7, 8, and 9
sequins in turn for a
graduated look.

6 At the base of the first
side, pass down through
the focal bead and the
size 5° triangles. Work a
second strand with 13
sequins. Pass back up the
strand. Make a knot
between the focal bead
and the size 5° triangle
and pass back down.

7 Work the third and final
strand with 10 sequins.
Work the second side
of the necklace in the
same way.

EARRINGS

1 Double-knot 40" (1 m) of
thread to an earring wire
leaving a 5" (13 cm) tail.

2 String 2 seed beads, 1
blue sequin, 2 seed
beads, and 1 green
sequin. Continue in the
same way adding sequins
in alternate colors until
24 are strung. Finish with
2 seed beads.

3 Count down 7 sequins
from the top. Pass
through the seventh
(blue) sequin. Pass back
up and attach to the loop
on the earring wire.

4 Finish ends.
➤ **Starting and finishing
threads, see page 138**

lotus flower

LARIAT AND EARRINGS

Brick stitch diamonds make this gorgeous flower. It's fixed to a screen finding clasp, along with the necklace and fringing. Work the diamonds with one bead at one end, and two beads at the other; the necklace will be easy to put together and remain very stable.

LARIAT

1 Work three brick stitch diamonds using 11 cream beads in the first row. Work four diamonds in beige and cream beads, using 10 beads in the first row. Work four peach diamonds, using 9 beads in the first row with an edging of dark peach.

2 Join the four peach diamonds at the two-bead ends. Secure adjacent diamonds using a square stitch halfway up, between the center outside beads of each.
▶ **Brick stitch diamonds, see page 121**

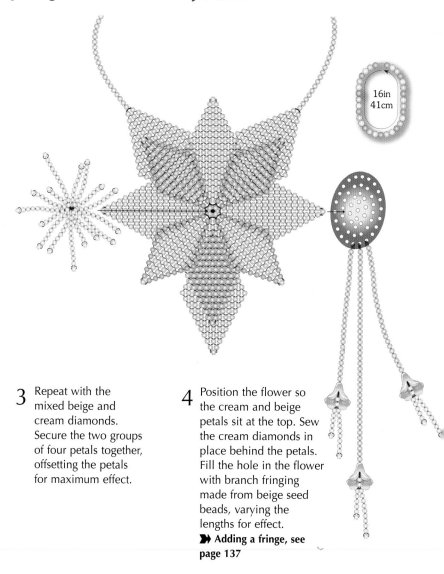

16in
41cm

Bead store

Lariat

10 g cream, beige, peach, and dark peach size 11° seed beads

5 g beige size 15° seed beads

3 acrylic flower head beads

Screen finding clasp with three places for attachment

Flat-nose pliers

Beading needle and thread

Earrings

5 g peach size 11° seed beads

2 g dark peach size 11° seed beads

2 g beige size 15° seed beads

2 acrylic flower head beads

Earring wires

Beading needle and thread

3 Repeat with the mixed beige and cream diamonds. Secure the two groups of four petals together, offsetting the petals for maximum effect.

4 Position the flower so the cream and beige petals sit at the top. Sew the cream diamonds in place behind the petals. Fill the hole in the flower with branch fringing made from beige seed beads, varying the lengths for effect.
▶ **Adding a fringe, see page 137**

5 Remove the screen disk from the clasp. Using the thread at the base of the flower, pass the needle back and forth through the screen holes to secure it. These stitches will be covered when the screen disk is clamped in place.

6 Tie 40" (1 m) of thread to one side of the clasp, leaving a 6" (15 cm) tail. String cream beads to the length required. Attach the single strand necklace to the bead at the point of the larger flower petal.

7 Weave the needle down and back up through the top half of the petal, passing the needle back through the single strand of beads. Finish off.
➤➤ **Starting and finishing threads, see page 138**

8 Repeat for the other half of the necklace.

9 Apply the three fringes to the bottom of your piece. Finish ends off.

EARRINGS

1 Using 40" (1 m) thread, work two brick stitch diamonds in peach with a dark peach edging. Work both diamonds down to 1 bead on each end.

2 Attach each finding to one end of a diamond.

3 Fold each diamond down the middle to judge where to attach the flower head. Pass the needle backward and forward through the diamond and the flower head bead to secure.

4 Work square stitch through the 2 central side beads to draw the diamonds together.
➤➤ **Square stitch, see page 125**

5 Pass the needle down 7 beads from the central beige bead. String 8 beige beads. Skipping the last bead, pass the needle back up through the next 7 beads added. Take it down through the next dark peach bead along, toward the point of the diamond.

6 Add four more strands of fringe, using 10, 12, 16, and 18 beige beads. Add another four strands, using 16, 12, 10, and 8 beads.

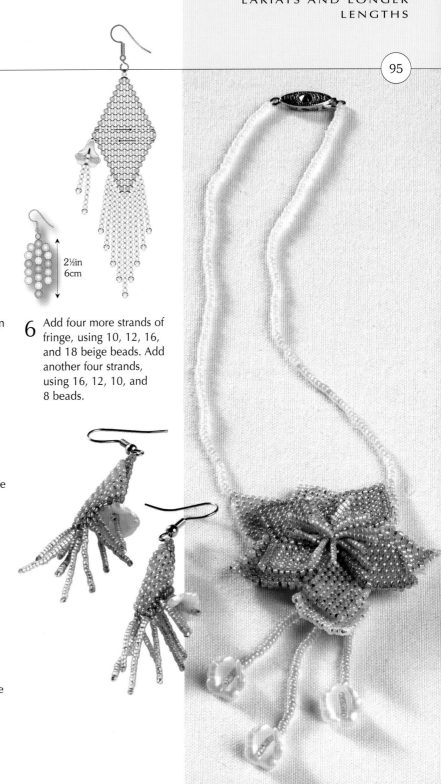

2½in
6cm

purples

NECKLACE AND EARRINGS

Simple and elegant, this necklace is suitable for any occasion, whether dressy or casual. It is long enough to go around the neck twice.

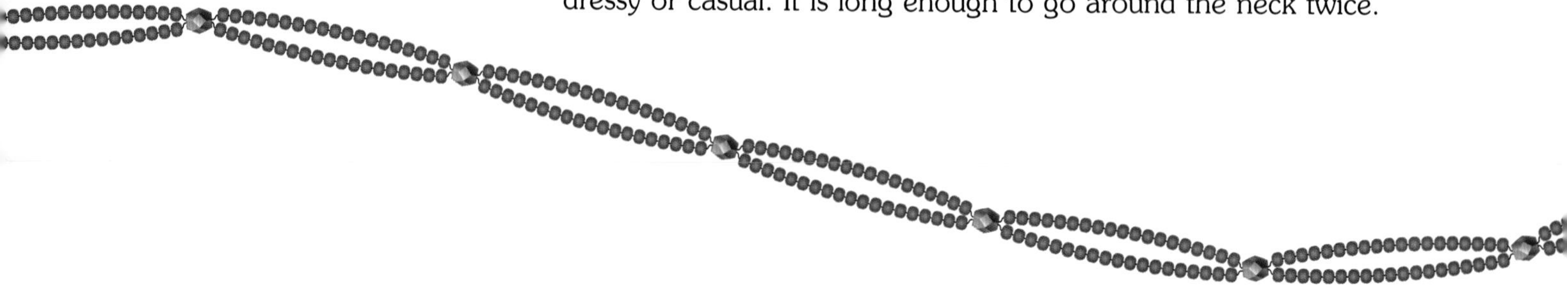

Bead store

Necklace

20 g matte purple size 11° seed beads

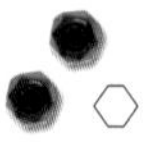

30 to 40 black 4mm fire-polished crystals

Beading needle and thread

22in
56cm

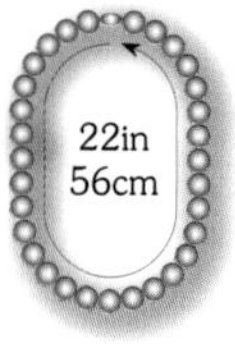

Earrings

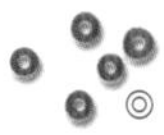

2 g matte purple size 11° seed beads

10 black 6mm fire-polished crystals

Earring wires

Beading needle and thread

NECKLACE

1 Using 60" (1.5 m) of thread, pass a seed bead down to within 6" (15 cm) of the tail end. Pass back up through the bead from the tail end to create a stop bead.

2 String 19 beads and 1 crystal, then * 20 beads and 1 crystal. Repeat from * until the necklace is the length desired.

3 Double-knot the ends together. Finish off the short ends.
➤ **Starting and finishing threads, see page 138**

4 Bring the needle out at the next crystal along for the second row. String 19 beads, then pass through the next crystal.

5 Continue to string 19 beads between each crystal until the necklace is complete. Finish off.

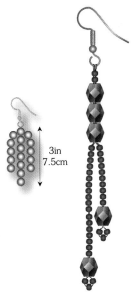

3in
7.5cm

EARRINGS

1 Double-knot about 40"
(1 m) of thread to one of
the findings leaving a 4"
(10 cm) tail.

2 String 2 seed beads, 3
crystals, 18 beads, 1
crystal, and 3 beads.
➤ **Adding a fringe, see
page 137**

3 Skip the 3 seed beads
and pass back up to
between the second and
third crystal from the top.
Knot around the core
thread. Pass back down
through the third crystal.

4 String 10 seed beads, 1
crystal, and 3 seed beads.

5 Skipping the final 3 seed
beads, pass back up
through all the beads
added. Double-knot
between 2 crystals. Pass
through a few more
beads. Trim ends.

6 Re-thread the tail end
and finish off in the same
way. Make another
earring to match.

sequins

NECKLACE AND EARRINGS

Sequins are the ultimate in party wear. This design makes the most of their sparkle and fun jewel-toned geometry as the light catches them. The earrings are made with 12 sequins and look great with the necklace.

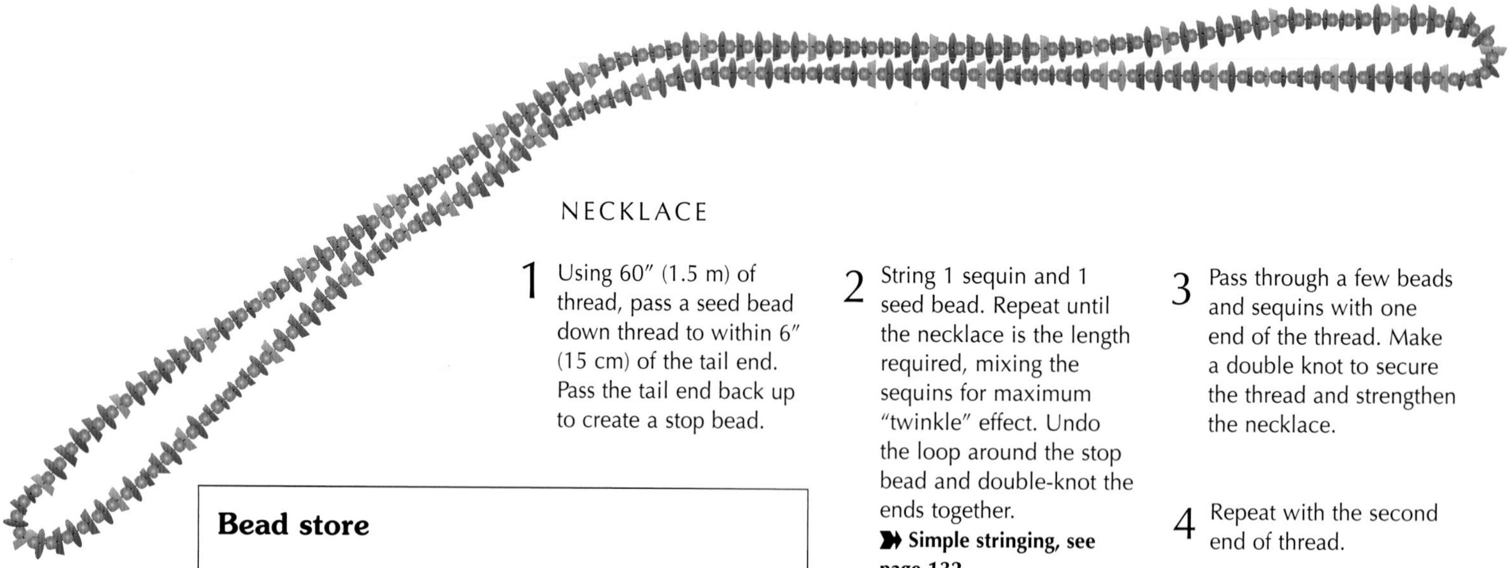

NECKLACE

1 Using 60" (1.5 m) of thread, pass a seed bead down thread to within 6" (15 cm) of the tail end. Pass the tail end back up to create a stop bead.

2 String 1 sequin and 1 seed bead. Repeat until the necklace is the length required, mixing the sequins for maximum "twinkle" effect. Undo the loop around the stop bead and double-knot the ends together.
➤ **Simple stringing, see page 132**

3 Pass through a few beads and sequins with one end of the thread. Make a double knot to secure the thread and strengthen the necklace.

4 Repeat with the second end of thread.

Bead store

Necklace

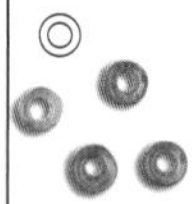

◎ 20 g blue-purple size 6° seed beads

20 g sequins in assorted sizes and colors

Beading needle and thread

22in
56cm

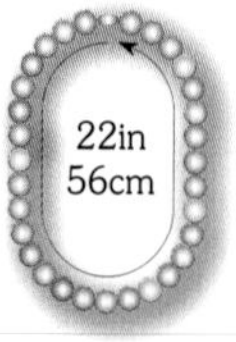

Earrings

5 g blue-purple size 11° seed beads

5 g multicolored sequins

Earring wires

Beading needle and thread

EARRINGS

1 Attach 24″ (61 cm) of thread to a finding, leaving a 5″ (13 cm) tail end.

2 String 3 seed beads, 1 sequin, and 3 beads. Repeat until 12 sequins are strung, increasing in size toward the center, and then decreasing to give the piece a graduated shape.

3 Add 3 seed beads at the base. Skipping the final bead, pass back through the length of the earring. Pass through the loop of the earring wire and back down into the beads. Double-knot between 2 beads. Pass through 2 or 3 more beads. Trim ends.
➤ **Starting and finishing threads, see page 138**

4 Finish the tail end off in the same way. Make another earring to match.

3½in
9cm

springtime blooms

——— NECKLACE AND RING ———

As near to wearing perfume without donning the real thing, this
necklace represents everything we love most about warm, sunny days.

NECKLACE

1 Double over 60" (1.5 m) of thread and pass both ends through the needle. Attach a clasp in the usual way.
➤ **Attaching a clasp, see page 140**

2 String 2 green size 11° beads, then size 6° beads for the first half of the necklace. String 1 focal bead, 1 size 6° bead, and 1 focal bead.

3 String 35 size 6° beads. Pass back through the first bead added to form a loop. Pass through the focal bead, 1 seed bead, the second focal bead, and the next seed bead.

4 String the second side to match the first. String 2 green size 11° beads. Pass through the other half of the clasp, the size 11° beads, and the first 5 size 6° beads.

5 String 2 size 11° green beads, 1 flower, and 1 pink bead. Pass back through the flower, the size 11° beads, and the next size 6° bead. String 1 green size 11° bead, 1 leaf, and 1 green size 11° bead. Pass back through the leaf, the size 11° bead, and the next size 6° bead.

Bead store

Necklace		**Ring**	
	15 g green size 6° seed beads		2 g green size 6° seed beads
	10 g green size 11° seed beads		6 green size 11° seed beads
	10 g pink size 11° seed beads		7 pink size 11° seed beads
	Assorted leaf and flower accent beads	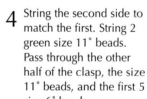	2 leaf accent beads
			2 flower accent beads

2 focal beads

Clasp

Beading needle and thread

12" (30 cm) pink elastic beading cord

23in
58cm

RING

6 String 10 pink beads. Pass back through the first bead added to form a loop. Pass through the next size 6° bead along.

7 String 3 pink beads, a flower, and a pink bead. Pass back down through the flower, the pink beads, and the next size 6° bead along.

8 String 10 pink beads. Pass back through the first bead to form a loop. Pass through the next bead along. Repeat Steps 5 to 8 to finish.

1 Cut the beading cord in half and put one length aside.

2 String size 6° green beads to fit the finger. Double-knot the ends to form a circle, pulling up tightly as you knot.

3 Double-knot the second piece of cord to the circle, as close to the knot as possible, so the two ends are equal. There should now be four lengths of cord ready to embellish.

4 Embellish two of the lengths by stringing 1 green seed bead, 1 leaf, and 1 green seed bead. Pass the cord back through the leaf and add 1 more green bead. Double-knot the cord around the core thread to secure.

5 Embellish the third length by stringing 2 pink beads, 1 flower, and a pink bead. Double- or triple-knot to secure.

6 Embellish the final length by stringing 2 pink beads, 1 flower, 1 pink bead, 1 flower, and 1 pink bead. Double- or triple-knot to secure.

7 Put a tiny dab of glue or clear nail polish over the knots. Let dry, then trim ends.

½in
1.25cm

opera

NECKLACE AND BRACELET

Classic colors make a classic necklace, which is easy to adjust in length and looks so dressy teamed with its matching bracelet. Spacer bars divide the bracelet into four sections and help to keep the strings in place. Use two strands of thread for a stronger bracelet.

NECKLACE

1 Using 60" (1.5 m) of thread, pass a seed bead down to within 6" (15 cm) of the tail end. Pass back through to create a stop bead. String a 4mm crystal, 2 seed beads, and a 4mm crystal.

2 String **1 seed bead, *1 bugle, and 1 seed bead. Repeat from * five times. String a 4mm crystal, a 6mm crystal, and a 4mm crystal. Repeat from ** five times as before.

3 String 1 seed bead and 1 bugle. Repeat seven times. String 1 seed bead, a 4mm crystal, and 1 seed bead. Pass back up through the crystal and the seed bead.

4 String 1 bugle bead to create a pair. Pass through the next seed bead along. Continue in the same way until you have applied 7 bugles. Pass through the next set of crystals.

5 Work five sections of bugles and seed beads for the second side of the necklace. String 5 seed beads and 5 bugles for the final section. String 11 size 11° seed beads and pass back through the first 2 beads to create a loop for the fastening.

6 Pass back down the necklace, adding a second row of bugles between the seed beads. Pass through the base crystal set again. String 5 bugles and 5 seed beads. Finish with a 4mm crystal and a seed bead. Skipping the last seed bead, pass back through the beads and the crystal set.

7 Make a knot around the core thread. Return and work the final fringing. Finish off, remembering to unthread the stop bead loop and tie off the threads.

Bead store

Necklace

 10 g crystal size 11° seed beads

 15 g matte black 6mm bugle beads

12 clear 6mm fire-polished crystals

 28 clear 4mm fire-polished crystals

Beading needle and thread

Bracelet

 200 to 250 fire-polished 4mm crystals

3 spacer bars with 5 holes

5-bar clasp

Beading needle and thread

13in
33cm

BRACELET

1 Make a paper cuff
template to determine
the size of the bracelet.
Double over 40" (1 m)
of thread and pass both
ends through the needle.

2 Pass through the top
opening on one side of
the clasp. Pass through
the loop and pull up to
secure.

3 Lay the crystals on the
template to determine
how many to use. You will
probably need 7 to 12
between each spacer bar.

4 String the beads. Pass
through the top opening
on the other side of the
clasp. Pass back through
2 or 3 crystals. Double-
knot between 2 beads.
Pass through 2 more
crystals. Trim ends.
➽ **Starting and finishing
threads, see page 138**

7in
18cm

5 String the remaining
four rows in the
same way.

earth tones

LARIAT

Amber beads endow this lariat with depth and warmth. It may take a while to plan how to use larger beads, but you really don't need many to make an impact.

Bead store

☐ 15 g warm brown size 6° seed beads

▣ Amber disk beads

Assortment of large beads in complementary colors

60" (1.5 m) waxed cotton bead cord

43in
109cm

1 Lay out the accent beads and try different combinations until you are happy with the effect. Tie a single knot at one end of the cord and pull to tighten.

2 String the beads, beginning with the last bead at one end. Mix in seed beads and use amber disk beads to "frame" the larger beads.

3 String the middle section using size 6° beads for comfort around the back of the neck.

4 Complete the second side to match.

5 Secure the last bead using a single knot at its base.

6 For extra security, add a small dab of glue or clear nail polish.

natural
NECKLACE

The natural tones of this necklace make it easy to wear with a wide-ranging palette of colors. Use size 6° beads for the neck section to make it comfortable to wear.

26in
66cm

Bead store

20 g size 6° seed beads in natural tones

5 g topaz size 11° seed beads

4mm disk beads in assorted natural tones

Focal bead

Clasp

Beading needle and thread

1 Double over 60" (1.5 m) of thread and pass both ends through the needle. Pass through one side of the toggle clasp. Pass through the loop and pull up.

2 String 4 size 11° seed beads. String size 6° beads for the first quarter of the necklace.

3 *String 7 disk beads in any combination, and 10 size 6° beads. Repeat from * to where the focal bead will sit.

4 String 7 disk beads, the focal bead, and 7 disks.

5 String 10 size 6° beads, 7 disks, and 3 size 6° beads. Skip the last 3 size 6° beads and pass back up through the disk beads and the next 10 size 6° beads. Bring it out between the sixth and seventh disks. Make a single knot around the core thread.

6 For the fringe, pass back down through the disk beads and 1 size 6° bead, string 4 size 6° beads, 7 disks, and 3 size 6° beads. Skipping the last 3 size 6° beads, pass back up through the fringe, 7 disks, focal bead, 7 disks, and the last of the 10 size 6° beads added before the central section.

7 To finish, string the second side to match.

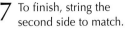

ceramic

NECKLACE AND EARRINGS

This easy-to-wear piece of jewelry combines ceramic focal beads and terra-cotta colored seed beads. The size 6° beads used for the back section make it more comfortable to wear. The earrings look great with the necklace.

NECKLACE

1 Double over 60" (1.5 m) of thread and pass both ends through the needle. Pass through one end of the clasp to form a loop. Pass through the loop and pull up to secure.
➤➤ **Attaching a clasp, see page 140**

2 String 5 size 11° beads, then string size 6° beads to form the back section.

3 String a larger terra-cotta bead, then 3 size 6° beads. Repeat almost to the center.

4 String the central focal bead and a size 6° seed bead.

5 For the first strand of fringing, string 20 size 11° seed beads, a size 6° bead, a large terra-cotta bead, and 6 size 11° beads. Pass through the first of the last 6 beads added. Pass back up through the rest of the strand and the heart. Make a single knot around the core thread. Pass through the heart.
➤➤ **Adding a fringe, see page 137**

6 For the second strand of fringing, pass through the size 6° bead directly below the heart. String 12 size 11° beads, a size 6° bead, a large terra-cotta bead, and 6 size 11° beads. Pass back through the first of the 6 beads just added, then the whole strand. Pass through the heart and the size 6° bead directly above.

7 Work the second half to match the first, finishing with 5 size 11° beads. Pass through the fixing point on the other half of the clasp. Complete as before.

Bead store

Necklace		Earrings	
	Large terra-cotta colored beads		6 terra-cotta size 6° seed beads
	15 g size 6° terra-cotta colored seed beads		5 g terra-cotta size 11° seed beads
	5 g size 11° terra-cotta colored seed beads		4 small heart accent beads
	Ceramic focal beads		2 medium cylinder glass beads
	Toggle clasp		2 earring wires
	Beading needle and thread		Beading needle and thread

25in
63cm

EARRINGS

1 Knot 40" (1 m) of thread to the loop of an earring wire, leaving a 6" (15 cm) tail.

2 String 3 size 6° seed beads, 1 cylinder bead, 1 size 6 bead, 3 size 11° beads, 1 heart bead, 15 size 11° beads, 1 heart, and 10 size 11° beads.

3 Bring the bead string round and pass through the size 6° bead, the cylinder bead, and the remaining beads up to the finding.
➤➤ **Beaded loops, see page 135**

4 Take the thread around the finding. Pass down through a few beads. Double-knot and pass through 2 or 3 more beads. Trim ends. Finish the tail end thread.
➤➤ **Starting and finishing threads, see page 138**

5 Work the second earring to match.

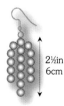

2½in
6cm

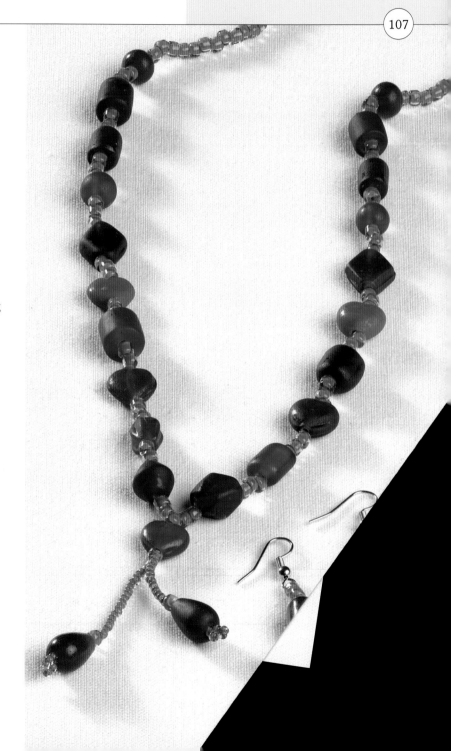

aloha

NECKLACE AND EARRINGS

The natural iridescent colors in the shells inspired this necklace, and the pretty bead loops add a flowery feel for an overall garland effect.

NECKLACE

1 Double over 60" (1.5 m) of thread and pass both ends through the needle. Pass through one end of the clasp. As a loop forms, pass through and pull to secure.

2 String in the sequence of 3 gunmetal beads, 1 bugle until the first half of the necklace is almost half the length required.

3 Pass the needle through from the back of 1 medium paua shell. String in the same sequence to fill the gap. Pass through the second hole and to the back. String in the same sequence for another 1½" (4 cm).

4 String the second shell as for the first. String in sequence to where the larger shell is to go. Pass through the holes, stringing gunmetal beads to cover the thread. Work to the last hole, turn.

5 Complete the second side in the same way. Apply the third shell so it sits below the last shell added on the first side. Apply the fourth shell so it sits between the first and second shell added on the first side.

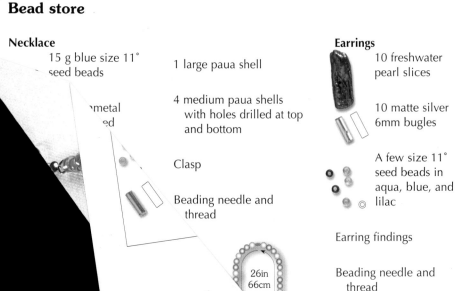

Bead store

Necklace

15 g blue size 11° seed beads

⸍metal ⸍d

1 large paua shell

4 medium paua shells with holes drilled at top and bottom

Clasp

Beading needle and thread

26in
66cm

Earrings

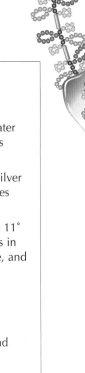

10 freshwater pearl slices

10 matte silver 6mm bugles

A few size 11° seed beads in aqua, blue, and lilac

Earring findings

Beading needle and thread

EARRINGS

6 String the second side in sequence to the length required. Pass the needle through the other half of the clasp. Turn and pass back through the 3 seed beads and the bugle.

7 Add four loops, one between each bead. Work the first and fourth loops in aqua with 5 beads in each. Work a loop in blue with 10 beads, and a loop in lilac with 10 beads. Pass through the next bugle along. Repeat until the necklace is covered.
➤➤ **Beaded loops, see page 135**

1 Knot 24″ (61 cm) of thread to an earring finding, leaving a 6″ (15 cm) tail.

2 String 1 bugle and 1 pearl slice. Repeat until you have 5 bugles and 5 slices in total.

3 String 10 blue beads. Pass back up through the last pearl slice. Make a single knot around the core thread. Turn and pass back down.

4 String 5 lilac beads. Complete a loop as before.

5 String 5 aqua beads. Complete a loop as before.
➤➤ **Simple stringing, see page 132**

6 Pass the needle back through several beads. Double-knot between 2 beads. Pass through 2 or 3 more beads. Trim ends. Pass the tail end through 2 or 3 beads. Finish off.
➤➤ **Starting and finishing threads, see page 138**

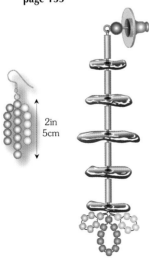

2in
5cm

BASIC TECHNIQUES

The final section of this book deals with the basic techniques. The off-loom techniques of peyote, brick, square, right-angle weave, herringbone, and netting stitch are covered together with full instructions for fringing, attaching clasps, and finishing.

Tools

AND MATERIALS

You will need very few tools and little equipment to begin designing jewelry. These are some of the essentials:

▲ Drill

These can be found at most hobby stores and are great for making holes in shells and stones.

▼▶ Beading thread

Many of the designs featured in this book were worked using Nymo, a flat beading thread made of nylon monofilaments. It is available in several sizes, but size D is the most common.

▼ Thread conditioner

Thread conditioner or beeswax is often applied to beading thread to help to prevent any knotting or splitting.

▼ Scissors

You will need a small pair of sharp scissors with points for trimming the ends of the thread.

◀ Nylon-coated beading wire

This was designed specially for stringing beads (see p.113), and is very flexible but also very strong. It comes in some great colors.

▶ Beading needles

These are available in many sizes and different lengths. The technique and personal preference will determine the length you choose. As a guide, size 10 is suitable for most projects, while the slightly finer size 13 is more suitable for techniques in which the thread passes through the beads several times.

◀ Clear nail polish

Clear nail polish can be applied to knots and left to dry before trimming the thread. This is an extra safeguard against the knot coming undone.

▶ Bead design board

This is really useful for placing beads when designing necklaces. It lets you look at several design options before making a final decision.

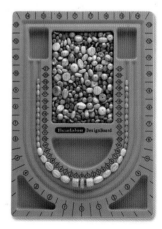

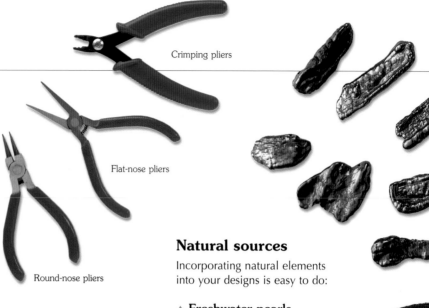

Crimping pliers

Cutting pliers

Flat-nose pliers

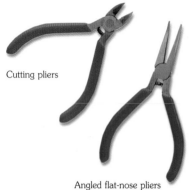

Angled flat-nose pliers

Round-nose pliers

▲ Pliers

Round-nose pliers
These have rounded, tapered points and are good for pinching and bending wire into shape.

Cutting pliers
These pliers should be sharp enough to give a good clean cut.

Flat-nose pliers
These pliers have a flat base with no ridges in the jaws for squashing or flattening sections of wire.

Crimping pliers
These pliers are used to clamp crimp beads to wire. They have recesses in the jaws that the crimp beads sit in as you clamp down on them.

Natural sources
Incorporating natural elements into your designs is easy to do:

▲ Freshwater pearls
These are available in many different shapes and dyed colors.

◄ Shells and slate slices
These can be bought or found on the beach. Beautifully smooth, flat slate slices are sometimes found on beaches in England. A small drill can be used to make holes in shells or slate slices.

▲ Agate slices
Agate slices come in many interesting shapes and sizes, and some are dyed in vibrant colors. They can be a fantastic challenge for the designer. Some are ready-drilled with holes.

Beads

Beads are available in so many different shapes, sizes, colors, and textures. At the beginning, the possibilities can seem a little confusing. These are some of the glass beads available:

▶ Bugle beads

These long, cylindrical tubes are available in several sizes including 4 and 6mm. Buy the best you can afford, as cheaper beads often have sharp, badly cut ends that will damage the working thread.

▶ Japanese cylinder beads

These small cylinder-shaped beads have extra-large holes and are very regular in shape. They are good for pictorial or pattern beadwork, as they sit so well together.

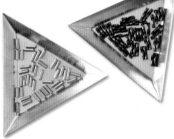

◀ Round, seed, and rocaille beads

The best, most evenly-shaped beads come from Japan and Czechoslovakia. These are used extensively in both loom and off-loom beading techniques.

▶ Hand-blown glass beads

These beads are individually hand-crafted and are often incorporated in free-form pieces of jewelry or strung simply to enhance their individual beauty.

▶ Triangle, cube, and hex beads

These are available in many sizes, finishes, and colors. They are good for textural work and strung applications.

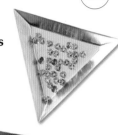

▶ Accent beads

These are wonderful to design with. From pretty flowers and leaves to animal print dagger beads, there is something for everyone.

peyote
STITCH

Peyote stitch is one of the most versatile and best-loved off-loom beadwork techniques. It is a flexible stitch that feels almost like a fabric. Thread tension plays a large part in its final appearance and texture. The stop bead is vital as it prevents the first row of beads from falling off the tail end, and allows the beadwork to be tightened as necessary.

Even-count peyote stitch

Beginners will find peyote stitch easier to achieve using an even number of beads. An odd count involves maneuvering the needle and thread through several beads to arrive in the right place and direction to start the next row, so should only be attempted once the even-count method is mastered.

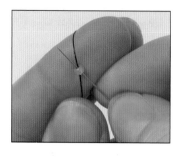

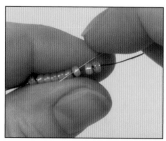

1 Thread a long beading needle with about 40" (1 m) of beading thread. String a seed bead to within 6" (15 cm) of the tail end. Pass back up through the seed bead to create a loop around this "stop bead." String 7 more seed beads in the same color.

2 String a seed bead in a second color. Let it rest next to the last bead on the first row, then pass through the next bead along on the first row. This will bring the newly added bead to the top of the first bead of the initial row, ready to begin the second row. String another bead. Skipping the adjacent bead in the first row, pass through the next bead in the row. Add 4 beads in total.

3 Look at the last completed row: The gaps between the beads are where the beads for the next row should be placed. If your work is a little loose at the end of the second row, and the beads are not sitting correctly, push the stop bead up toward the other beads using your thumbnail.

4 String another bead in the first color and let it rest on top of the stop bead. Pass through the next bead along, which will be sitting slightly above the initial row of beads. Continue in the same way to the end of the row. At this point you may find it easier to flip your beadwork over.

5 Pick up a bead and let it sit on top of the first bead of the row beneath. Pass through the next bead along, which will be sitting slightly above. Continue to the end of the row. Add rows until you are confident working the stitch.

Flat circular peyote stitch

This variation of peyote stitch produces a flat, circular piece of beadwork, ideal for lids or to cover the bottom of vessels. When you first practice this technique, use seed beads in two different colors to highlight each new row so the pattern of the beads can be followed more easily.

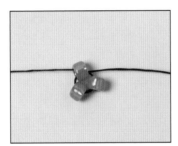

1 String 3 seed beads and push them down to within 6" (15 cm) of the tail of the thread. Pass through the 3 beads again to form a circle.

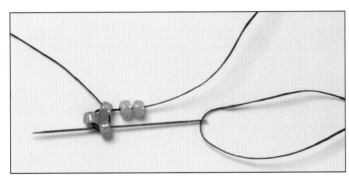

2 To begin the second row, add 2 seed beads between each bead of the first row. Step up by passing through the first bead on the previous row, then through the first bead of the first pair of beads added on this row.

3 Add a seed bead between each bead of the previous row, including 1 bead between each pair from the last row. To step up, pass through the first bead added on the last row, then through the first bead added on this row.

4 For Row 4, add 2 beads between each bead of the previous row. Step up by passing up through the first bead on the previous row, then through the first pair of beads added on this row.

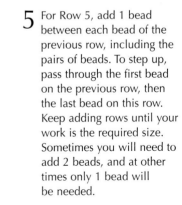

5 For Row 5, add 1 bead between each bead of the previous row, including the pairs of beads. To step up, pass through the first bead on the previous row, then the last bead on this row. Keep adding rows until your work is the required size. Sometimes you will need to add 2 beads, and at other times only 1 bead will be needed.

Tubular peyote

Tubular peyote creates a hollow tube, and can be worked around any cylindrical object, such as a drinking straw or length of dowel. A clear drinking straw is ideal when you first attempt the stitch, as it lets you see your work.

When working this stitch, you can start off with either an odd or an even number of beads. If using an even number, you will need to step up at the end of each row. This is the best method when creating a pattern or pictorial piece. If using an odd number, you will just spiral up to the next row. The example shows even-count working. It is exactly the same as flat even-count peyote, but is worked in a tube.

2 String one bead and let it sit above the next bead along. Pass through the third bead along from the start of the initial row of beads. Pull slightly as you take the thread through the bead so the two beads sit nicely one on top of the other. Continue along the row in this way until you return to the first bead added.

1 String an even number of beads and tie in a double knot around a tubular object, leaving a tiny gap between the first and last bead in the circle. Do not overlap the beads or the stitch will not lie correctly and will be impossible to work. Take the needle back through the first bead again.

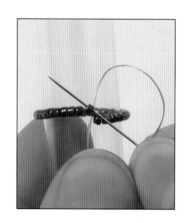

3 To step up, pass through both the first bead of the initial row and the first bead of this row. Add rows in the same way until you reach the required length.

Note to beaders

Before embarking on a project featuring peyote stitch, it is always wise to try a sample piece first. This will help you to perfect the tension, especially if you are new to the stitch.

Peyote spirals

This is a versatile technique, and interesting results can be achieved using different sizes of beads. Forty beads should create about 3″ (7.5 cm) of spiral, depending on how tightly you work. Work a small section using 40 beads, measure and multiply to obtain the required length.

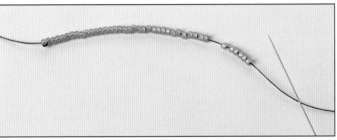

1 Using 40″ (1 m) thread, string 1 size 11° seed bead down to within 6″ (15 cm) of the tail of the thread. String 39 more beads.

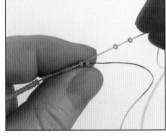

2 Work a second row of peyote stitch in the same color, but add 2 beads instead of 1 above every other bead of the first row.

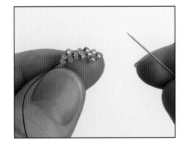

3 Work loosely and let the pairs of beads splay apart. Do not worry if they do not all sit on the same side of the initial row.

4 Before you start Row 3, pull slightly on the stop bead to keep it from sliding away.

5 Using another color, work a third row of peyote stitch adding 1 seed bead between every bead of the second row (including the pairs of beads). This row makes the spiral form, so keep your work firm. As you work, maneuver each pair of beads to the right side of the beadwork using thumb and forefinger.

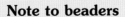

Note to beaders

Continue to add rows of beads using single beads and pairs of beads alternately, or use larger beads. The possibilities are endless!

6 Depending on individual tension, 10 beads will create approximately ¾″ (2 cm) of spiral. It is a good idea to work a small section first to check, then you can multiply the beads for the required length.

ladder

STITCH

Ladder stitch is used widely as a starting point for both brick and herringbone stitch.

Starting the ladder

This first step forms the foundation row for brick stitch. It can be worked with either bugle or seed beads, depending on your choice of project. Using bugles is a good way to familiarize yourself with the stitch since they create a more stable ladder than seed beads.

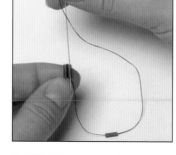

4 Thread on a third bugle and take the needle back through the second bugle, from top to bottom.

1 Thread a long beading needle with 60" (1.5 m) of beading thread. Pick up 2 bugle beads and slide them to within 6" (15 cm) of the tail end of the thread. Take the needle back through the first bugle.

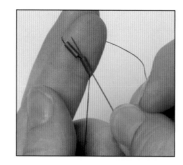

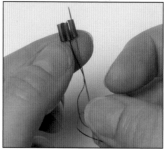

5 Pull the thread through and down toward the tail end until the third bugle sits against the second bugle. Thread back up through the third bugle.

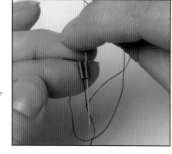

6 Continue adding bugles in the same manner until the foundation row reaches the required length. Notice that you are alternating between taking the needle through the top and bottom of the previous bugle added.

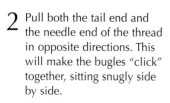

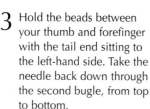

2 Pull both the tail end and the needle end of the thread in opposite directions. This will make the bugles "click" together, sitting snugly side by side.

3 Hold the beads between your thumb and forefinger with the tail end sitting to the left-hand side. Take the needle back down through the second bugle, from top to bottom.

Note to beaders

Remember not to thread your needle through the side of the bead your working thread is protruding from.

brick
STITCH

Brick stitch, also known as *Comanche* stitch, after the Native American peoples, is a much more solid stitch than many of the other widely used techniques. If you look at a flat piece of brick stitch you will see that it resembles a brick wall, hence the name.

1 Using size 8° seed beads, work a bead ladder 7 beads across.

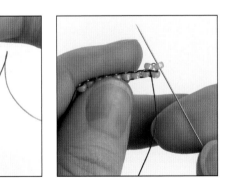

2 String 2 seed beads.

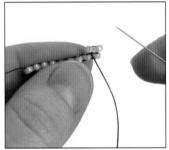

3 Pass through the first loop of the initial bead ladder from back to front, letting the 2 beads sit side by side with the holes pointing upward.

4 Pass back up through the first bead.

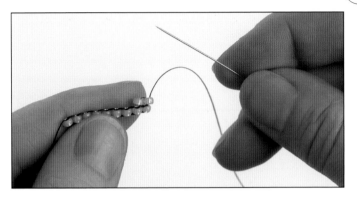

5 Pass down through the second bead.

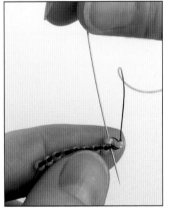

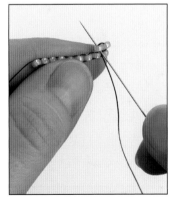

6 Pass through the loop of the initial bead ladder again.

7 Turn the needle and pass back up through the second bead.

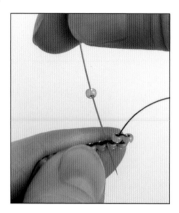

8 String a third bead and pass through the next loop along the initial bead ladder.

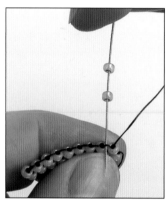

10 Turn the work around and pick up 2 beads to begin Row 3.

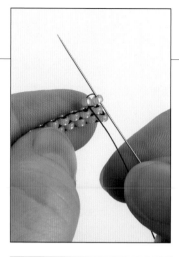

11 Pass through the last loop of the first row of beads, letting the 2 new beads sit side by side, holes upward.

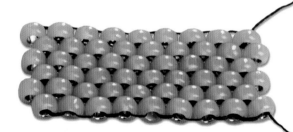

12 Pass back up through the first bead, down through the second bead and the first loop again, then back up through the second bead. Work to the end of the row, adding 1 bead at a time as before.

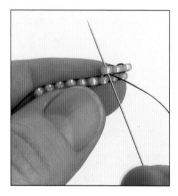

9 Pull the thread through the loop until the bead sits next to the previous beads. Pass back up through the bead and pull gently upward until all 3 beads sit in a row. Continue working along the row, 1 bead at a time.

Note to beaders

The first five steps produce what is known as the "locking" stitch. Work a locking stitch at the beginning of each row. This will help to anchor the first bead and stop it tipping inward, keeping your work flat and even.

13 The finished stitch.

Decreasing on the outside edge

Decreasing on the outside edge to form diamonds is relatively simple. Instead of passing the needle through the first loop of the last row, it is passed through the second loop which moves the beads inward.

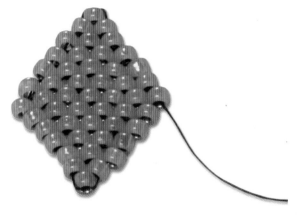

1 At the beginning of the row you wish to decrease, string 2 beads, but this time pass through the second loop in from the end of the previous row. Pass back up through the first bead, then down through the second bead, the same loop, then back up through the second bead again. Continue along the row adding one bead at a time as before.

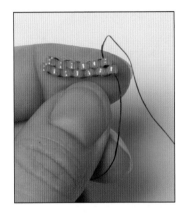

2 To begin the next row, pick up 2 beads. Thread through the second loop in from the end of the previous row.

3 As more rows are added, the beadwork will decrease to a point. Pass back down through the beadwork to one of the outside beads on the initial row. Complete the other side in the same way to create a diamond shape.

Note to beaders

The locking stitch at the beginning of each row is important when decreasing. This ensures that although the beads are moving inward the outside bead still sits up straight and creates a tidy edge.

netting

STITCH

Netting stitch became particularly popular in Victorian times, but it originated in ancient Egypt. The stitch produces an open, lacy effect that drapes beautifully around the neck or wrist. It can also be worked firmly enough to make a tube.

This technique is the basis of all netting stitches; only the number of beads used varies. This example was worked using size 11° seed beads in red and black, but you can use any color.

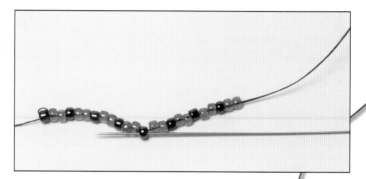

2 Pass back up through the twelfth bead (black), from the bottom. Pull up to form the first diamond. There should be a black bead at all four points of the diamond.

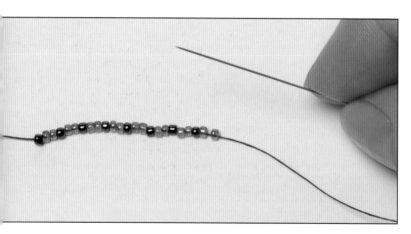

1 Thread a long beading needle with 40" (1 m) of beading thread. String 1 black seed bead and slide to within 6" (15 cm) of the tail end. Pass back up through the bead, to create a stop bead. String 2 red, 1 black, and 2 red beads until 24 beads in total are strung, including the stop bead.

3 String 2 red, 1 black, and 2 red beads. Count up 5 beads on the original row and thread up through the sixth (black) bead.

4 Make another diamond in exactly the same way as in Step 3, finishing the row by passing back up through the stop bead.

5 String 2 red, 1 black, and 2 red beads again. Take the needle down through the center black bead of the last diamond on the previous row.

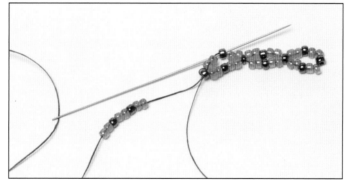

7 String 2 red, 1 black, 2 red, 1 black, and 2 red beads. Pass back up through the center black bead of the last diamond on the previous row. The netting pattern will begin to emerge. Add rows until your work is the required length.

6 String 2 red, 1 black, and 2 red beads. Pass down through the second center black bead of the previous row to form another diamond. Repeat to make another diamond.

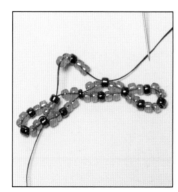

Note to beaders

To ensure that the beadwork sits evenly when working netting stitch, do not pull the thread too tightly.

Tubular netting stitch

Tubular netting makes interesting necklaces and bracelets, and one netted tube can be worked over another for an impressive effect.

1 String 1 black and 2 red beads until there are 15 beads in total. Wrap the beads around a drinking straw and tie in a double knot. Pass through the first black bead again.

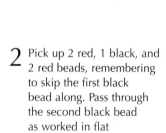

2 Pick up 2 red, 1 black, and 2 red beads, remembering to skip the first black bead along. Pass through the second black bead as worked in flat circular netting.

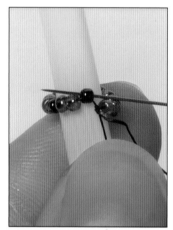

3 After forming the second loop only 1 black bead will remain to attach the third loop to. As the stitch spirals, you should pass through the black bead of the first loop added on this row, which effectively is the step up. Continue to add rows until the desired length is reached.

Note to beaders

Working this stitch over a drinking straw helps to keep the tension constant throughout.

An example of tubular netting stitch on a finished piece (see Blue Bead Necklace, page 25).

square

Square stitch beadwork is easily mistaken for work produced on a loom. The two techniques are similar in appearance, but the advantage of square stitch is that there are no ends to weave in as with loom work.

Cylinder beads are often used with this stitch for two reasons: The first is that they are uniform and sit next to each other perfectly. Secondly, the central holes are fairly large for the size of bead, which makes it easier to accommodate the amount of thread that needs to pass through each bead. For this example, size 11° cylinder beads were used.

1 Thread a long beading needle with about 60" (1.5 m) of beading thread. String a seed bead and slide it to within 6" (15 cm) of the tail end. Bring the needle back up through the seed bead to create a stop bead. String 9 more beads.

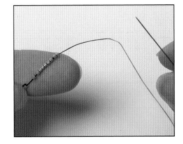

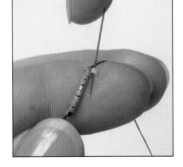

2 Pick up a bead and pass back through the previous bead on the row (thread goes in a circle).

3 Turn the needle and pass back through the bead just added.

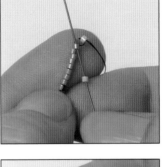

4 Pick up a bead and pass back through the second from last bead of the first row.

5 Turn the needle and pass back through the bead just added. Continue to add individual beads and work along the row, passing through the adjacent bead on the previous row and back through the bead just added.

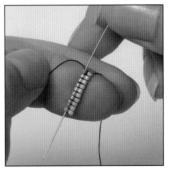

6 At the end of the row the beads may seem to be sitting slightly unevenly, so they need to be secured together. To do this, pass back through the first row of beads, then turn and pass back through the second row. Follow Steps 2 to 6 to add rows.

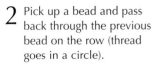

Note to beaders

This is one of the easier stitches to keep the tension right. Once you have been through the first two rows with your thread, you can begin the stitch.

herringbone
STITCH

Herringbone stitch has endless possibilities, as you will see when working through the various samples. With this stitch, increasing and decreasing can create some wonderful shapes and textures. Experiment with differently shaped beads and you could make some great discoveries.

Ladder stitch start method for herringbone stitch

This starting method is ideal for beginners. Size 8° seed beads in two colors have been used for the following steps so the thread and bead patterns can be easily identified when working. Eight beads is a good size for a practice piece.

3 Bring the needle up through the third bead in the ladder row.

4 String the next pair of beads in the second color and pass down through the fourth bead along on the foundation row. Gently pat the 2 new beads until they sit side by side with the holes facing upward. Complete the row in the same way.

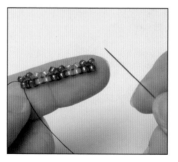

5 As the second row is worked the herringbone or chevron effect will begin to appear, with each pair of beads tilting slightly toward each other. At this point the beads will be sitting in matching pairs, and the next row will connect them.

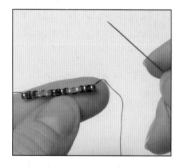

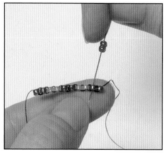

1 Work a ladder stitch foundation row (see page 118) using size 8° seed beads in pairs of each color.

2 String 2 beads in the first color, to match the pair at the end of the initial row. Pass down through the second bead along on the foundation row. Pat the 2 new beads gently so they sit side by side with the holes facing upward.

6 The thread is now trailing from the first bead of the original ladder row. The next moves take the working thread so that it emerges from the left-hand bead of the first pair of beads. Pass up through the second bead along on the original ladder.

7 Now take the thread across and up through the left-hand bead of the first pair on Row 2.

8 For Row 3, string a pair of beads to match those directly below. Pass through the second bead of the first pair of beads on Row 2.

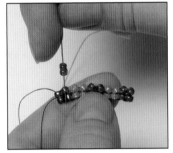

9 Come up through the first bead of the next pair along on Row 2 to create the "linking" stitch between each pair of beads.

10 String 2 beads in the second color and bring the needle down through the right-hand bead of the pair below, on Row 2.

11 Pass up through the first bead of the next pair along on Row 2 and continue along the row in the same manner.

12 Repeat the diagonal move to enable Row 4 to begin. You will notice from the finished row that the thread is not in the correct place to begin the next row. Pass back up through the next bead on Row 2, then through the right-hand bead of the first pair on Row 3. Work Row 4.

13 Continue building up rows in the same way.

Note to beaders

Remember, when linking the pairs together you are only threading up and down through the row you are working on, not two or three rows below it.

Tubular herringbone stitch

This stitch makes an attractive tube suitable for a necklace or bracelet. Try working this technique with size 5° triangle beads in two contrasting colors. The tension takes a little time to master, but is well worth it.

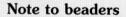

1 Work a ladder stitch foundation row (see page 126) using 6 size 5° triangle beads. Form a circle with the holes of the beads pointing upward. Join by passing through the first and last triangles on the ladder several times.

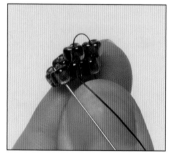

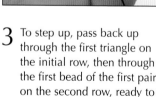

4 Pick up 2 beads and pass down through the left-hand bead of the second row.

5 Pass up through the first bead of the next pair along. This is your linking stitch. Continue to add rows to reach the required length.

2 String 2 triangles in a contrasting color. Pass down through the next bead along on the initial row, then up through the third triangle along. Repeat, adding 2 more pairs of beads.

3 To step up, pass back up through the first triangle on the initial row, then through the first bead of the first pair on the second row, ready to start Row 3.

Note to beaders

Start to hold the tube between your thumb and forefinger as soon as you can to encourage the beadwork upward. Always pull upward on the thread when working.

right-angle
WEAVE

Right-angle weave is one of the most versatile and fluid bead weaving stitches. It is named because the beads sit at right angles to each other. Increasing and decreasing changes it to fit over almost any shape. It is worked in groups of four beads that link together to form a chain effect, and the thread travels a circular path that gives it great flexibility and texture. The stitch can also be worked using groups of three beads on each of the four sides, which gives each link a square effect. This is often referred to as "square netting."

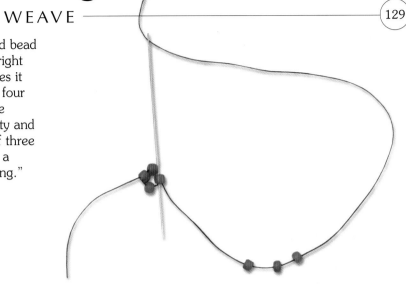

1 Thread a beading needle with about 40" (1 m) of beading thread. String a bead and slide it down to within 6" (15 cm) of the tail end. Pass back up through the seed bead to create a stop bead.

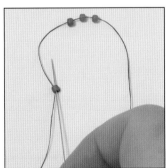

2 String 3 seed beads. Pass back through the first (stop) bead, the second, the third, and the fourth beads again. Pull up into a flat circle.

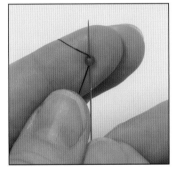

3 String 3 more seed beads. Pass back down through the bead that the working thread is emerging from.

4 Pass through the next 2 beads along. The thread should be passed through at this point to allow the next set of beads along the chain to be worked. Take a moment to work out which bead the thread should emerge from.

5 String 3 more beads and come back up through the bead the thread is trailing from. Pass through the next 2 beads along. Continue in the same way until six bead "circles" have been worked.

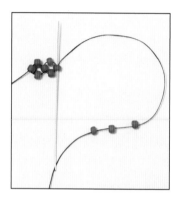

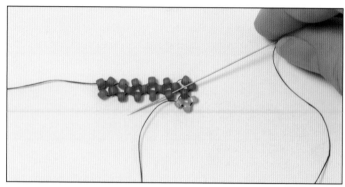

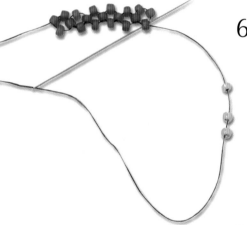

6 For the next row, add the last set of 3 beads as usual, then pass through the next bead along. String 3 beads and pass back through the bead the thread is trailing from. Pull up to form a flat circle.

7 Pass back through the 3 beads just added, then through the bottom bead of the next chain of the original row.

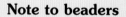

8 String 2 more beads. Pass through the 2 beads already in place, then through the first of the 2 beads just added.

Note to beaders

The thread must always be worked in alternating circles, never straight up or down. If it crosses these diamonds either vertically or horizontally the thread path is incorrect. If this is the case you will also notice a stiffening of the beadwork.

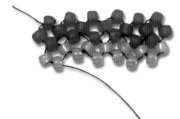

9 Continue along the row in the same way. Small diamonds will form between the first and second rows.

Square right-angle weave

This technique is worked in exactly the same way as the basic stitch (pages 129–130), but using groups of three beads on each side to form squares.

1 String 1 bead and pass back through it to form the stop bead. String 11 more beads. Pass through the first set of 3 beads again.

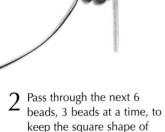

2 Pass through the next 6 beads, 3 beads at a time, to keep the square shape of the beadwork.

3 String 9 beads. One side of the second square is already in place; pass down through the 3 beads that form the square wall again.

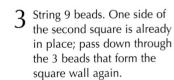

4 Pass through the next two sets of 3 beads to reach the correct position for the following square. Continue in the same way until the beadwork is the desired length.

5 To add the next row, bring the needle just through the 3 base beads of the square. String 9 beads and pass back through the beads the working thread is trailing from.

6 Pass back through all the beads just added, then through the bottom 3 beads of the next square along on the original row. Continue in the same way to complete the row.

Note to beaders

Always thread through three beads at a time to encourage squares to be formed.

simple
STRINGING

One of the easiest and fastest ways to create a simple strung necklace is with nylon-coated beading wire, knot cups, a split ring, and lobster clasp. Simple stringing can also be done using beading thread and cord, according to the look you want.

1 Using a bead design board, arrange your chosen beads.

3 Pass the wire through the "hinge" of the knot cup.

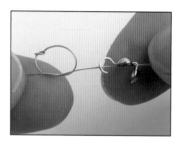

4 Tie a double knot at the point where you want it to sit.

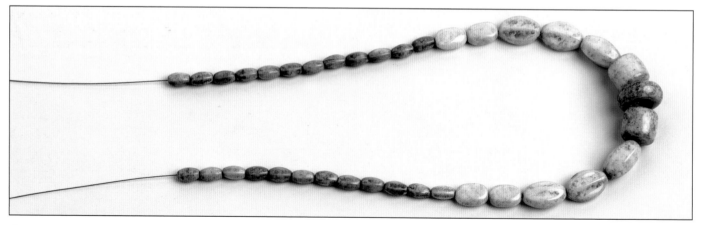

2 Cut the required length of nylon-coated wire, allowing an extra 6" (15 cm) for the knot cups and clasp. String the beads.

5 Trim the wire and dab clear nail polish on the knots.

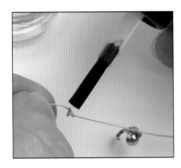

6 Pass the thread through the knot cup until the knots rest between the two halves of the cup.

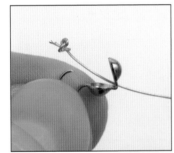

7 Using round-nose pliers, clamp the two halves of the knot cup together.

8 The clamped knot cup.

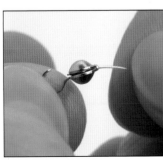

9 Place the lobster clasp on the open loop.

10 Using round-nose pliers, join the loop.

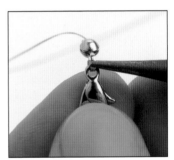

11 Repeat Steps 4 and 5 for the other side, adding the split ring to the knot cup to complete the fastening.

Note to beaders

The key to simple stringing is forward planning. Take time choosing your beads and use a bead design board to try different combinations.

working with
METAL FINDINGS

Memory wire

This is an almost-instant way to create chokers and bracelets. It is great for beginners and a good way to introduce children to making jewelry. To finish the ends, you can apply drilled beads using a dab of glue, or you can bend the wire round to form a loop that stops the beads escaping.

1 Take one end of the memory wire and place it between the jaws of flat-nose pliers.

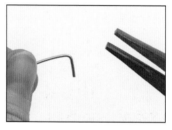

2 Bend the wire down 45 degrees.

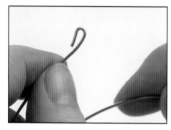

3 Change your grip and bend the wire back on itself to form a loop. String the beads on the wire, leaving ¼" (6 mm) of wire at the other end. Finish as before.

Drilling

Often you will find really special pieces of shell or minerals that are not pre-drilled with holes. It is easy to drill holes using a small model-makers' hand drill. Hold firmly between a vise or your fingers.

Crimping

Applying crimp beads needs a certain amount of practice, and a good pair of crimping pliers. It does not matter if the "crimp" is not perfect as long as it holds the beads securely and does not scratch the skin.

1 String on a crimp bead, the beads between, then a second crimp.

2 Holding the wire, place the crimping pliers over the crimp bead, resting in the second notch. Squeeze the pliers down on the crimp bead to secure in place.

3 Using thumb and forefinger, hold the beading wire in place. Attach the second crimp as you did the first.

Flat leather crimps

1 Place the end of the cord into the flat leather crimp.

2 Using round-nose pliers, bend one side over, then bend the other side over the top of the first flap. The cord is now secure. Add jump rings and a lobster clasp to finish (see page 132).

branch fringing
AND BEADED LOOPS

When you add branch fringing it is best to be quite adventurous with color, shape, and texture, or the piece will just end up looking like a mass of beads. Shaping is also important, so place the longest strand at the center and graduate gently to short lengths at the ends of the piece.

1 Bring the needle out of the bead where you wish to add the strand of fringe. String the required number of beads.

2 Skipping the last bead added, pass back through the beads, emerging where you wish to add a side strand (which can be any length you like).

3 String the required number of beads. Skipping the last bead added, pass back through the beads just added.

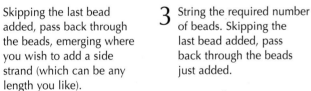

4 Pass back into the main body of the strand.

5 Pass through to the next bead where you want to add a strand of fringe.

Note to beaders

Always pull up the loops correctly so that no thread is showing between the loop and the line of core beads.

Beaded loops

1 String the required number of beads for the loop. Before returning to the main body of the beadwork, pass back through the first seed bead of the loop.

2 Pass through the next bead along of the core beads.

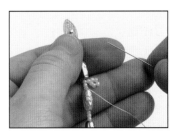

3 The finished loop.

picot
EDGING

Picot edges are great fun and easy to do. Several different effects can be achieved, depending on how many beads you use. If you use just three beads little points appear, whereas five beads makes a wavy frill. Using an accent color for the center bead produces a great effect. Picots can be added to the edges of bracelets, to clothing, bags, and earrings, and to the top of amulet purses—the list is endless. Beaded loops also look good as an edging. These are worked in the same way as picots, but leaving gaps between the loops.

Picot points

1 Bring the needle out through the bead where you wish to position the picot. String 3 size 11° seed beads, then take the needle down through the next bead along.

Picot loops

1 Bring the needle out through the bead where you wish to position the picot and string 5 or 7 size 15° beads. These are particularly effective for creating picots.

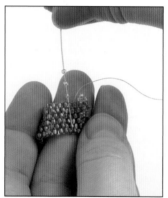

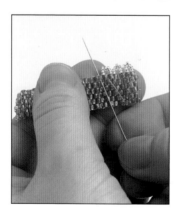

2 Pass the needle up through the next bead along, ready to begin the second picot.

2 Take the needle down through the next bead along, then pass through the next bead ready to start the second picot. Continue beading until all the picots are worked.

Note to beaders

Loops can be very effective when crossed with each other or intermingled.

adding a
FRINGE

Fringing adds a lovely finishing touch to bracelets, necklaces, bags, and earrings—in fact, almost anything. It creates movement in the piece, and allows you to incorporate a woven or colored pattern if you wish. For the best results, remember these important points:

Dangle factor
Hold the work up to check it as each strand of fringe is added. If the thread is too loose it will show and the beads will not sit snugly. If it is too tight, the fringing will buckle and pull, spoiling the effect.

Fringe patterns
If you plan to add a pattern to the fringe, it's a good idea to work out the design using graph paper and colored pencils.

Choice of beads
It is a good idea to lay out the beads you plan to use. If you want to place an accent bead at the base of each strand, "step" them so they do not bang into each other. Work straight or shaped fringes as you please. If you include bugle beads, make sure they are not badly cut, or they will sever the thread and your work will be lost.

Positioning the fringe
When adding a fringe to a necklace, use one of these methods:

1 Find the center of the necklace then add the fringing from the center out to the furthest strand on one side. Repeat for the other side.

2 Count out from the center to the outermost strand of fringe on one side. Beginning at the side, complete the fringe by working straight across.

Note to beaders
The "dangle factor" is the most important thing to check when creating a fringe.

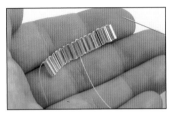

Adding a fringe

1 Anchor a fresh length of thread into the main body of the beadwork, passing the needle down until you reach your starting point.

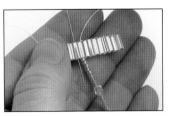

2 Thread the beads required for the first strand of fringe, and slide them down toward the beadwork.

3 Pass back up through all the beads except for the last 3 (which allows you to pass back up the line of beads, and also add a decorative finish to the end of the fringing).

4 Pass the needle back up through the bead you initially emerged from in the main body of beadwork.

5 Pass through the next bead along, ready to work the second strand of fringe.

starting and finishing

THREADS

There are several ways to start and finish off threads, and everyone has their favorite, so choose which works best for you. Here are two different methods:

Weaving threads

On woven pieces, when the working thread is down to 6" (15 cm) long it can be woven into the beadwork. Change direction several times so the thread will not work loose, and cut the end off as close as you can to the work. Add a new piece of thread in exactly the same way. It may be best to attach the new thread before finishing off the old piece, especially with stitches such as peyote, as it saves any confusion about where you should continue.

Knotting

1 When the working thread reaches 6" (15 cm), remove the needle. Thread up a fresh length of thread. Begin to pass the needle diagonally up from the bead the working thread is emerging from.

2 Pass the needle through 2 or 3 beads. Bring it out, then work a double knot between the 2 beads, taking the needle beneath the thread.

3 Pass through the next few beads until the thread is emerging from the correct bead. Give it a slight pull as you work. You will be aware of a slight click as the knot moves into the next bead along, which will hide it completely.

4 Return to the original working thread and finish off in exactly the same way, taking the thread back down through the beading in the opposite direction.

Note to beaders

Don't worry about the knot showing between the beads. It will disappear into the next bead along when the thread is pulled through.

knotting

BETWEEN BEADS

Knotting between beads produces an attractive appearance, and also adds strength to a piece. It prevents larger ceramic beads from grinding together and being damaged with chips and sharp edges. It is often easier to begin a knotted necklace in the center. Remember to allow yourself plenty of extra cord for the knots.

The "stop" bead

A "stop" bead is not counted as the first bead of a pattern. It has two functions: To stop the beads falling off the tail end of the thread, and to provide a stable starting point which can be moved if necessary to tighten the work. Use either a large contrasting bead or one similar to beads you are using in your work. When the work is complete, either remove the stop bead, or—if the bead is part of the design—undo the loop around it.

The basic technique

1 Make a single knot just off the center of the necklace. Work a second knot directly over the first.

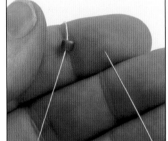

2 String the bead you wish to capture between the knots. Begin to tie the first knot of the second side, but before you begin to pull it up, place a large tapestry needle in the center. This will allow you to move the knot along until it sits right next to the bead.

3 Still holding the needle in position, begin to tighten the knot. At the last moment, pull the needle away and pull the knot up firmly. Work a second knot over the top of the first.

1 Thread the needle as normal. Pass the stop bead to within 6" (15 cm) of the tail end.

2 Pass through the bead from the tail end upward, ready to begin beading.

Note to beaders

Take time when positioning the second knot over the first and make sure that the bead sits snuggly between the knots.

attaching
A CLASP

Adding the correct clasp to a finished piece of jewelry sets it off perfectly. Always buy the best clasp you can afford. With all the time and effort put into creating a piece, it deserves a great finish!

Toggle clasps

A toggle clasp consists of a ring and a T-bar, each with an eye or point for threading through. Five size 11° seed beads should be added to both ends to allow enough ease for the T-bar to pass through the clasp.

1 Using about 80" (2 m) of thread, pass the two ends through the eye of the needle, leaving a loop at the bottom of the thread. Pass through the eye of the ring end of the clasp.

2 Secure by passing through the loop of thread just before the loop goes through the eye.

3 Pull the doubled thread up firmly to secure to the ring section of the clasp.

4 String 5 size 11° seed beads. String beads to the required length, then string 5 more size 11° seed beads.

5 Add the second half of the toggle in exactly the same way.

Bar clasps

These keep beadwork flat and are good for cuff bracelets and choker necklaces.

Place the clasp by the finished edge of the piece to align the beads with the clasp eyes. Bring the needle out through one of these beads, then pass through the corresponding eye. Pass back through into the main body of beadwork. Repeat several times. Attach the other side of the clasp in the same way.

Simple clasps

Pass the working thread through the center bead on the end of your beadwork. Pass through the eye of one half of the clasp, then back into the main body of the beadwork, turn. Repeat this step three to four times until the clasp feels secure.

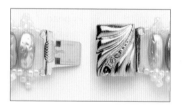

Note to beaders

Bar clasps should always be attached to the nearest seed bead sitting opposite each end of the clasp.

bead and
LOOP FASTENERS

Bead and loop fasteners are a popular way to finish pieces of jewelry. They look particularly good on a flat design like a Victorian collar. They can become an integral part of the necklace, especially if you use a bead that matches beads in the main necklace.

Bead fastener

1 When the necklace is the required length, pass through the center bead at the end of your work. Using a color that matches or complements your work, string 3 size 11° seed beads to form a stem for the loop.

2 Pass the fastener bead down toward the 3 seed beads.

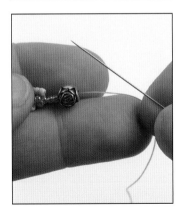

3 String another seed bead, turn the needle and pass back through the larger bead and the 3 seed beads again. Pass back into the body of the work, turn, then pass back two or three times more from the bead fastener into the body of the work to secure. To finish, make a double knot, then pass the needle through 2 or 3 more beads. Trim thread.

Loop fastener

1 Make a stem of 3 seed beads as before. String size 11° beads to the length required to make the loop large enough to slip over the bead fastener.

2 Pass back down the stem and into the body of the work. Turn. Pass around the loop then back down the stem two or three more times to secure. Finish off as before.

Note to beaders

As an alternative when working a fairly plain rope, you could use the fastening bead to make a statement.

index

Seed beads and general beading supplies:
Out on a Whim
121 E. Cotati Ave.
Cotati, CA 94931
(800) 232-3111
www.whimbeads.com

Pressed glass and general beading supplies:
Beadcats
PO Box 2840
Wilsonville, OR 97070-2840
(503) 625-2323
www.beadcats.com

Semiprecious stones and general beading supplies:
Fire Mountain Gems
One Fire Mountain Way
Grants Pass, OR 97526-2373
(800) 355-2137
www.firemountaingems.com

Swarovski crystals and pearls:
Crystal Beads of Boston
31 Hayward St., Ste. A-1
Franklin, MA 02038
(866) 702-3237
www.crystalbeadsofboston.com

Sequins:
Cartwright's Sequins & Vintage Buttons
11108 N. Hwy. 348
Mountainburg, AR 72946
(479) 369-2074
www.ccartwright.com

Screen findings:
Ornamentea
509 N. West St.
Raleigh, NC 27612
(919) 834 6260
www.ornamentea.com

Ceramic pendants:
Marsha Neal Studio
PO Box 1560
Hockessin, DE 19707
(302) 559-6781
www.marshanealstudio.com

Author acknowledgments

All my love and thanks go to Grant, who took over family life and "did" everything, allowing me time to put this book together. Thanks also to all at Quarto, especially Kate Kirby and Liz Pasfield for their support and encouragement throughout.

Dream Home

INNERFORMSLTD.COM